FOREX TRADING INVESTING FOR BEGINNERS

Pen Name:
(Matthew Swing)

Matthew Swing

© Copyright 2021 - All rights reserved.

The content contained within this book may not be reproduced, duplicated or transmitted without direct written permission from the author or the publisher.

Under no circumstances will any blame or legal responsibility be held against the publisher, or author, for any damages, reparation, or monetary loss due to the information contained within this book. Either directly or indirectly.

Legal Notice:

This book is copyright protected. This book is only for personal use. You cannot amend, distribute, sell, use, quote or paraphrase any part, or the content within this book, without the consent of the author or publisher.

Disclaimer Notice:

Please note the information contained within this document is for educational and entertainment purposes only. All effort has been executed to present accurate, up to date, and reliable, complete information. No warranties of any kind are declared or implied. Readers acknowledge that the author is not engaging in the rendering of legal, financial, medical or professional advice. The content within this book has been derived from various sources. Please consult a licensed professional before attempting any techniques outlined in this book.

By reading this document, the reader agrees that under no circumstances is the author responsible for any losses, direct or indirect, which are incurred as a result of the use of information contained within this document, including, but not limited to, errors, omissions, or inaccuracies.

Table Of Contents

INTRODUCTION 10

CHAPTER 1: TECHNICAL AND FUNDAMENTAL ANALYSIS 14
- FUNDAMENTAL ANALYSIS 14
- TECHNICAL ANALYSIS OF FOREX TRADING 16

CHAPTER 2: FOREX TRADING STRATEGIES 22
- SWING TRADING 23
- INTRADAY TRADING 25
- POSITION TRADING 25
- NEWS TRADERS 26
- TREND TRADING 26
- END OF DAY TRADING 27

CHAPTER 3: CURRENCIES EXPLAINED 28
- THE MAJOR CURRENCY PAIRS 28
- EUR/USD 28
- USD/JPY 29
- GBP/USD 29
- USD/CHF 30
- USD/CAD 30
- AUD/USD 31
- NZD/USD 31
- CROSSES 31
- EXOTIC CURRENCY PAIRS 33

CHAPTER 4: HOW TO CONCRETE START WITH FOREX TRADING WITH PRACTICAL EXAMPLE – STEP BY STEP 34
- STEP 1: THINGS TO LOOK FOR WHEN SELECTING AN FX DEALER 34
- STEP 2: HOW TO OPEN A FOREX TRADING ACCOUNT 35
- STEP 3: WHEN CAN YOU BEGIN TRADING 36
- STEP 4: SOME WELL-KNOWN FX DEALERS 36
- STEP 5: SPREADS 37

CHAPTER 5: HOW TO TRADE WITHOUT EMOTIONS 38
- BE PATIENT 38
- BE OBJECTIVE 38
- BE DISCIPLINED 39
- BE REALISTIC 39
- 1 TRUST THE PROCESS 39
- 2 OUTLINE DAILY ACTIVITIES 40

3 Analyze the Market 40
4 Be Defensive 40
5 Have A Trading Plan 41
6 Know That Trading Is A Business 41
7 Outline Risk 41
8 Use Technology 42
9 Have A Stop Loss 42
10 Focus on The Bigger Picture 42
11 Keep Learning Markets 43
12 Be A Progressive Trader 43

CHAPTER 6: HOW TO "WIN" FOREX MARKET AND CREATE PASSIVE INCOME – STEP BY STEP GUIDE 44

Making Passive Income In The Forex Market 44
Understanding Forex Quotes 44
Determining to Buy Or Sell 45
Bid and Ask Price 45
Time to Make Money 45
EUR/USD Pair 46
USD/JPY 46
USD/CHF 46
Pips and Pipettes 47
What Is Leverage? 49
Market Order in Forex 50
Types of Orders 50
Limit Entry Order 50
Stop-Entry Order 51

CHAPTER 7: MONEY MISTAKE TO AVOID 52

Avoid the Get Rich Quick Mentality 52
Trade Small 52
Be Careful With Leverage 53
Not Using A Demo Account 53
Failing To Check Multiple Indicators 54
Use Stop Loss and Take Profit Orders 54
Remember Price Changes Are In Pips 55
Don't Try Too Many Strategies or Trading Styles At Once 55
Market Expectations 55
Have Fun 56

CHAPTER 8: PERSONAL RECOMMENDATION 58

Tips For Success 58

CHAPTER 9: RISK AND MONEY MANAGEMENT 62
BUDGETING FOR PROFIT 62
RISK MANAGEMENT 63

CHAPTER 10: HOW TO SET-UP YOUR FOREX TRADING ACCOUNT AND BEGIN TRADING 68
GEARING UP WITH A FOREX PRACTICE ACCOUNT 68
SETTING UP A FOREX TRADING ACCOUNT 69
TRADING LEVERAGE 69
FEES AND COMMISSIONS 70
OTHER FACTORS 71
HOW TO START TRADING IN THE FOREX MARKET 71
ORDER TYPES 72

CHAPTER 11: TOOLS FOR FOREX TRADING 74
IG 74
SAXO BANK 74
CMC MARKETS 75
TD AMERITRADE 75
FOREX.COM 75
CITYINDEX 76
XTB 76
DUKASCOPY 76
FXCM 77

CHAPTER 12: SECTOR ANALYSIS AND STRATEGY 78
RANGE TRADING STRATEGY 78
TREND TRADING STRATEGY 80
PAIRS TRADE 80
PRICE ACTION TRADING 81
CARRY TRADE STRATEGY 81
MOMENTUM TRADING 82
PIVOT POINTS 83

CHAPTER 13: WHAT A BEGINNER NEEDS TO KNOW ABOUT FOREX TRADING . 86
WHICH QUALITIES MAKE YOU AS THE BEGINNER SUCCESSFUL IN THE TRADING 88

CHAPTER 14: WHAT DO YOU DO IF THE MARKET IS GOING IN THE WRONG DIRECTION? 92
PAY ATTENTION TO DAILY PIVOT POINTS 92
DEFINE TRADING STYLE AND GOALS 92
TRADE WITH AN EDGE 93
THE TRADING PLATFORM AND BROKER 94

PRESERVE CAPITAL... 94
  SMALL LOSSES AND FOCUS 95
  SIMPLE TECHNICAL ANALYSIS 95
  WEEKEND ANALYSIS 96
  PLACING STOP-LOSS ORDERS AT THE RIGHT PRICE LEVELS............................. 96
  USE A CONSISTENT METHODOLOGY 97
  CHOOSING THE RIGHT ENTRY AND EXIT POINTS... 97

CHAPTER 15: THE RIGHT APPROACH 100

  THE IMPORTANCE OF A TRADING PLAN 102

CHAPTER 16: CHOOSING A BROKER 104

  LIST OF COMMON BROKERS 104
  SIGNS OF ILLEGITIMATE BROKERS 108

CHAPTER 17: BENEFITS OF FOREX TRADING 110

  LIQUIDITY 110
  TIMING 110
  RETURNS 110
  COSTS 111
  NON-DIRECTIONAL TRADE 111
  MIDDLEMEN ELIMINATED 111
  NO UNFAIR TRADE 112
  NO ENTRY BARRIER 112
  CERTAINTY 112
  EASY INFORMATION 112

CHAPTER 18: TIME MANAGEMENT AND MONEY MANAGEMENT 114

  TIME MANAGEMENT 114
  MONEY MANAGEMENT 116

CHAPTER 19: HOW IS FOREX TRADING BENEFICIAL TO THE FINANCIAL MARKET? 120

  FOREX AND THE WORLD 120
  HOW CAN BANKS INTERVENE WITH FOREX RATES? 123
  FOREX INTERCESSIONS COME IN TWO TYPES: 124

CHAPTER 20: PIPS AND WHAT YOU NEED TO KNOW ABOUT THEM 128

  WHAT IS A PIP? 128
  WHAT IS THE FUNCTION OF THE PIP? 129
  POPULAR CURRENCY PAIRS IN TRADING 130
  HOW DO I CALCULATE PIPS? 131
  WHY IS IT IMPORTANT TO UNDERSTAND PIP 133

CHAPTER 21: MISTAKES AND TIPS FOR BEGINNERS IN FOREX TRADING 136
- Forex Mistakes 136
- Tips for Trading Forex 136

CHAPTER 22: HOW TO MAKE MONEY WITH FOREX TRADING TO CREATE PASSIVE INCOME 140
- Forex Signals 141
- Forex Robots 141
- Social Trading 142

CHAPTER 23: COMPOUND INTEREST AND FOREX 144
- Using The Power Of Compound Interest 145
- The Secret Of Paying Of Yourself First 145
- The Maths Behind Compound Interest: An Easy Example 147

CHAPTER 24: THE RESISTANCE TRADING STRATEGY 152
- Exchange Traded Funds (ETFs) 156
- ETFs Versus Mutual Funds 156
- Types Of ETFs 157
- Examples And Up-To-Date Tips 158

CHAPTER 25: PRACTICAL GUIDE TO THE TREND-LINE 160
- Trading Strategy With The Use Of RSI 164

CHAPTER 26: CURRENCY FUTURES AND CRYPTOCURRENCIES 168

CHAPTER 27: EASY WAYS TO REDUCE YOUR RISKS 174
- Research the Economies You Want to Invest In 174
- Keep the Emotions at Home 175
- Work with a Broker 175
- Put Your Stop Losses in Place 176
- Never Revenge Trade 177
- Find a Mentor to Work With 177
- Take a Break When Needed 178
- Do Not Invest with More Than You Can Afford to Lose 178

CONCLUSION 180

BONUS CHAPTER 182
- Forex Robots 182
- How To Program The Metatrader 4 To Automate The Management Of Operations With A Custom Trading Console 183
- Machine Learning For Algorithmic Trading 186
- Day Trading diary 188

Introduction

The first thing you need to understand about the Forex market is that it is purely speculative which means that when a Forex transaction is completed, there is nothing that is actually changing hands. Instead, the entire market, such as it is, exists as little more than numbers in a database that are then tallied to determine if your total is in the black or in the red. This is because the Forex market only came into being as a way for major corporations with offices all around the world and other global powers to take care of various expenditures without having to worry about trading currencies in the traditional sense.

Instead, they make their transactions via the forex market and everyone else speculates on how their moves are going to affect the market. In general, about 20 percent of forex transactions are made by these major entities while the rest are all investors who are hoping to make a little profit in the interim. Of this 80 percent, 80 percent are professional traders while the rest are just individuals like you.

Unlike in other markets, when a forex trader commits to a trade, they are trading a pair of currencies rather than shares of a single asset. As such, due to its very nature every forex transaction involves buying a certain amount of one currency while also selling a certain amount of a second currency. Currencies are typically trade in a few different amounts. First of all, a micro lot is 1,000 units of a currency so $1,000 is a micro lot of dollars. Finally, a standard lot is the name given to 100,000 units of currencies which means that $100,000 is a standard lot of dollars.

Additionally, the smallest amount that a currency can move on the forex market is referred to as a pip. 1 pip equals a single percent of the total amount of the currency. When you are first getting started as a forex trader it is important to start with micro lots as when they move a pip your investment only moves 10 cents. This means that you don't necessarily need to be at the top of your game all the time at first and builds you in some natural resistance to failure. If you purchase a mini lot, then you stand to lose a dollar per every pip of negative moment and with a lot you will lose $10. Remember, currencies can often move 100 pips or more in a single day and never invest more than you can afford to lose.

While it might sound dramatically different than the more commonly seen markets available, the forex market is driven by the same primary forces as the stock market, namely supply and demand. This can be seen every time the world decides that it needs more of one specific type of currency; when this occurs, prices of that currency rise. This will continue up until the point that the market once again becomes oversaturated with that type of currency and the prices starts to move back in the other direction. The best way to keep tabs on this sort of thing Is by reading reports from world powers, rumors of geopolitical strife and the current interest rate.

What further separates it from other types of investment markets is the fact that rather than reopen and close every single day, is the fact that the forex market is only ever closed from Friday night until Monday morning. While this means the market as a whole never sleeps, it doesn't mean that all of the types of currencies are traded at a single time, rather, the market is broken up into three chunks, the United States, Europe and Asia. While there is some overlap at the edges, a majority of the trading during those hours is going to be focused around pairs of currency that feature one of the currency pairs of the region in question. As an example, if you were interested in trading the US dollar then you would want to ensure you were available to do so during the American part of the day.

While there are numerous different currency pairs from all around the world, there are just 18 that are considered by most to be of the greatest importance. While this doesn't mean that you should try and trade all of the pairs at once, it does mean that you will need to be aware of them and what they are doing so you have a better forecast of the market as a whole. Even better, the 18 pairs are all from just 8 countries. While this doesn't make successful forex trading any easier, it will make it easier when it comes to knowing where to put your focus.

CHAPTER 1:

Technical And Fundamental Analysis

Fundamental Analysis

Fundamental analysis is a financial market analysis method to know the price movements and predict the future outcome of the prices of the asset in the market. Fundamental analysis in forex trading has its focus centered overly on the economy.

The analysis also researches on a variety of factors that affect the forex trade as well as how the elements affect the national currency value. Various factors influence the economy, and these include interest rates, employment, unemployment, GDP, international trade, and manufacturing industries.

In fundamental forex analysis, the price of the may differ from the value of the same asset in the market. Prices may vary because of various factors, and because of the difference in the price and the value of the asset, different markets underprice or overprice the demands for a short period. However, the fundamental analysts believe that despite the value of the assets being underpriced, mispriced, or overpriced in the short period, and it always goes back to its original correct price after some time. The main objective of any fundamental forex analyst is to get the right price and value of the asset, compare the two, and finally come up with an opportunity to trade.

Fundamental analysis is very different from technical analysis. Fundamental analysis does not pay a lot of attention to the current price like the technical analysis. The fact is that fundamental analysis is not an excellent analysis tool for intraday traders in forex trading.

Forex fundamental analysis has many different theories that try to explain it and make it a suitable analysis tool for forex trading. The most common approach is economic theory. This theory attempts to explain that the price conditions should be exchanged when they are adjusted. It summarizes that this exchange should be done according to the local economic factors.

Major Economic Indicators

The economic data in the market shows the movement of the economy of different countries. A trader who wants to invest should be very keen on commercial change. The major economic indicators show the price movements, comparing it to their values giving the traders opportunities of finding new trading chances to invest and profit.

Inflation

Inflation is the balance between the circulation of money in economic growth and distribution. Each country or market has a set level of which the rise can reach. There is a healthy inflation level and unhealthy inflation level. When inflation is high in any economy, supply and demand are disturbed. Supply gets an advantage because there is more than what is demanded. This high inflation affects the currency negatively. The currency drops. Oppositely, when inflation is low- deflation, there is more demand than supply. During this deflation period, money value rises, and the cost of goods go down in the market. It is a strategy that most economies employ but on a short-term basis. If deflation strategy is used long term, it will have adverse effects on the economy. The responsible party will get a hard time stabilizing their economy again.

Gross Domestic Product (GDP)

Gross Domestic Product of a country is the sum of all the monetary value of all goods and services of a given country within a specific time frame. This monetary value of the goods and services must be produced within the borders of that same country. A country's Gross Domestic Product is calculated annually, although there is a possibility of calculating it quarterly depending on the countries policy concerning the GDP calculation.

Gross Domestic Product is the best economic indicator among other economic indicators. Most people think GDP can never be an indicator because it only measures the market value of the goods and services, but they are wrong. From forex fundamental analysis view, when there is an increase in a gross domestic product without an increase in the demand of the products, this constitutes to a weak economy.

Interest Rates

There are different types of interest rates, but the main focus of fundamental forex analysis falls on the nominal and the base interest rates. The central banks of different states set these interest rates. The central bank has to lend money to private banks after creating money. Therefore, the interest amount paid by the private banks on the loans they have acquired from the central bank is called the nominal interest. The nominal interest rate is also known as the base interest rate.

Advantages of Fundamental Analysis

Show the trend of the market price.

Can be an excellent and reliable indicator, especially when it is combined with the technical analysis. It can work out for long term trades.

Technical Analysis of Forex Trading

When price patterns change from one to another, causing a change of prices in the market, these patterns have a specific way of doing so. When changes in price patterns in markets are studied and mastered to help in the prediction of future price patterns, this is now called the technical analysis. Most traders prefer using technical analysis over fundamental analysis. However, some traders use both the analysis techniques. Technical analysts use a different method to analyze the price patterns in markets. The techniques used include:

Chart Patterns

These are patterns where the prices are drawn on charts inform of graphs. When data is drawn on the graph, there is always a repetitive pattern. This pattern shows the movement of the prices in the forex markets. It shows the strength and the weakness of the trade. Some forex traders use the chart patterns as continuation signals or the reversal signals. The technical analysts using this chart patterns use horizontal lines, trend lines, and the Fibonacci retracement level to find the signals of the chart patterns. The chart patterns show the strengths and weaknesses of the forex market.

Horizontal Lines

These lines are also called sideways trends. These lines connect the lows and the highs in the variables. In this case the prices on the charts. These lines show the price that is below the support level and above the resistance level.

Trend lines

Trend lines are lines drawn on the chart or the graph to show support or resistance. These trend lines are dependent on the direction in which the prices are going in the forex trade. They are also known as horizontal support and resistance. When analysts are using trend lines in the chart patterns, they can see the increase or decrease in supply and demand.

The traders make up their mind whether to invest or not when this increase or decrease occur. When the prices are going up, it is called an upward trend, and the forex traders can sell. When the prices are going down, it is called a downward trend, and buyers can make their entry in the trade.

Fibonacci Levels

These levels in chart patterns exhume the hidden support and resistance. The support and resistance can be hidden due to the golden ratios. The origin pf Fibonacci is from the mathematical proportion, but it acts like the old support and resistance in the chart patterns when the price levels are laid out.

Candlestick Patterns

Forex technical analysts use to find the open, high, and low-price levels in the markets (OHL). The prices sought must be of a specific period in the trading session so that a comparison of the trader's behavior during the trade is made against the prices at that particular time. This analysis will help in predicting the future price movement in the forex trade market.

Technical Analysis Indicators

The technical forex analysts use the price action indicator. These indicators include;

The moving average

The moving average indicator shows the averages of prices in a given period. The moving averages display the direction of the market. The moving average helps balance the prices in the market by removing the unwanted prices. This removal helps the trader focus on the trend of the prices in the market. There are four types of the moving averages, namely the exponential moving averages (EMA), simple moving averages (SMA), linear weighted average (LWA), and the smoothed averages.

Bollinger Bands

This indicator is a tool used in technical analysis that comprises of three lines. These lines are plotted positively and negatively but away from the simple moving average of the currency price. These lines are adjustable to the trader's preference. The Bollinger bands help measure the variation degree of prices during the trade. In simpler terms, it measures the volatility of the market in a given period. The Moving Average Convergence Divergence (MACD)

This price indicator shows the momentum of the market. It shows when the market is doing well or not and the force behind this action. While using this indicator, a signal will always be evident is a market is moving in one direction. The Moving Average Convergence Divergence indicator belongs to a class of oscillators. Oscillators are technical indicators too and shown separately, below the prices in the charts.

Technical analysis has principles that should be followed

Principle of Technical analysis

Price Moves according to trends

Technical analyses assume that the prices in the trend move according to the trend patterns. The prices move in a bullish trend, bearish trend, and the sideways trend.

All price movements repeat themselves

The theory in this principle called the Dow Theory assumes that the price of a commodity represents its actual value, and it does not have to look at other factors. The principle claims that the prices in the patterns are repetitive and any future price is likely to be the same as the current price.

Advantages of Technical Analysis

Shows the Trend of the Market

Technical analysis shows the traders direction of the market. They can know the time the downward movement of prices and the upward movement, hence enabling them to make to sell or buy at the appropriate time.

Shows the trader Both Entry and Exit points

Timing is essential to a person trading in the forex. Poor timing will cause significant losses, and which will cause the trade to fail. The technical analysis predicts the time for investment for traders. It gives traders the upper hand to know when entering the trade or exit that trade.

Different indicators in technical analysis aids traders get the advantage of knowing investment time early. The candlesticks, moving averages, chart patterns, trend lines, and other indicators help in the calculation of the entry and the exit time in the trade.

Technical Analysis is fast

Technical analysis is fast in giving information about a specific trade. This action makes it quick and reliable to short term traders like the intraday traders who trade in one minute to thirty minutes. In this trade, candlestick patterns are used.

Technical Analysis Gives Adequate Information

Short term traders use technical analysis, swing traders, and long-term traders. Enough information is found in the chart patterns, and forex traders can use this information to their advantage. The traders can pursue their trades utilizing this information and get satisfying returns. More details like the trading psychology, market momentum, volatility, support, and resistance are a portion of the vital information that the technical analysis provides.

Technical Analysis is Cheap

Technical analysis of software's is cheap. Some software's are free offers from different charting software companies, and they can even be downloaded on mobile apps.

CHAPTER 2:

Forex Trading Strategies

When you are trading a financial asset, you are going to have some wins, and you are going to have some losses. When you are a beginner, you might have more losses than wins if you don't put any time in to study how the markets work. Many beginners simply trade on the fly, going with their gut feelings. This is not a productive way to go about trading, and it can end up wiping out your account. When this happens, many traders simply give up and stop trading.

The goal of a trading strategy is to use proven methods to help you get more wins than losses. This can be combined with your knowledge of candlestick charts and what the indicators are telling you. It can also be combined with fundamental analysis. This is a term most frequently used in the stock markets, where fundamental analysis means studying the fundamentals of the company.

In the case of Forex markets, fundamental analysis is probably going to mean examining macro-economic factors. You are going to be checking how healthy a given economy is. You'll look at the GDP growth rates, the trends, and job creation numbers, for example. You are also going to want to look at the central bank policy, and what the current interest rates are. Trade and other factors are going to be important. Fundamental analysis will give you an overall idea of how strong a currency is relative to other currencies. However, fundamental analysis isn't really a strategy; it's more like another tool. So you can put it in the same category as candlesticks and indicators.

There are many different trading strategies. One of the things that you will need to consider before trading is the time frame over which you want to operate. Many traders want to trade over very short time frames, taking smaller profits over short-term and usually smaller price moves. Others prefer to go long term, holding positions for days or even weeks (beware of interest rate risk).

There is no right or wrong answer to this question. So you have to try it, and possibly research it to determine what the best time frames are for you to use. This is a matter of personal style, and it's possible to make profits using any time frame. Some people find a longer time frame to be something that can generate a large amount of anxiety.

Day trading or holding a position for a few hours is not something that appeals to everyone either. If you are following a short-term trading strategy, one of the consequences of this is that you must pay close attention to the markets. You will have to be constantly checking to see how your investment is performing and look to the right time to exit the trade. And you will have to exit your trades very quickly. This can put a lot of stress on people, some are well-suited for it, but others may not be. In addition, it simply requires a commitment of time. Some people simply don't have the time to stare at their computer screens for hours on end. Of course, one advantage of the Forex market is that it runs 24 hours a day. This has major practical implications, and if you are too busy in the daytime because of a commitment to a job, you can do short-term trading strategies in the evening.

With that in mind, let's consider some of the main trading strategies that are used in the Forex markets.

Swing Trading

Swing trading is a simple idea to describe. If you are a swing trader, you will buy positions at the bottom of a downtrend. Then you will sell positions at the top of an uptrend. Of course, the trick is actually recognizing when the bottom of a downtrend or top of an uptrend actually occurs. This will require a solid knowledge of charting. You will watch a downtrend, and during this process be looking out for signals indicating a coming price reversal. When you see the signals, then you buy the currency pair.

Note that if you are talking about a currency pair A/B, you might have "sold" the currency pair in a bet on currency B rising against currency A. That means that in this case when you buy, you are actually exiting or closing your position.

But if you are betting on currency A, this is the point at which you enter the position.

Then you will ride the trend as long as you can. You can have an automatic order placed to exit when the price rises to a pre-determined level, or you can watch the charts for signals of a new trend reversal, that would take the currency pair A/B into a trend that is heading back down.

If you would prefer trading over a longer time period, swing trading is a trading style or strategy that might be to your liking. The idea behind swing trading is relatively simple. You look for price swings that take place over the course of days or weeks. Many Forex traders tend to be impatient, and if that is you, then you might not be suited for swing trading. As a swing trader, you are going to be required to hold your positions at least overnight. Some swing trades may involve holding a position for several weeks.

In some ways, swing trading is a more relaxed style of trading. You aren't sitting in front of your computer screen sweating bullets, waiting for the exact moment to exit the trade and take your profits. Instead, you might be checking the position only periodically.

However, swing trading cuts both ways. The Forex markets are highly volatile, and so this means that there are going to be a lot of short-term ups and downs. It requires a great deal of fortitude to wait these short-term price movements out. Some people actually find swing trading to be more stressful. For example, you might have bought the currency pair A/B, and so you are betting on A rising against B over a longer time frame. But you might see the price of the A/B pair drop considerably on its way to the higher price point. This is something that is important to be aware of because some people simply don't have the willpower to stick out a trade, when it appears to be going badly. But keep in mind that prices fluctuate all the time on Forex. It's unlikely that a price decline is going to be something that can be said to be a permanent thing. For the swing trader, it's a matter of simply waiting it out.

Intraday Trading

Intraday trading is another day trading style, but it's more relaxed than scalping. So you are looking to enter and exit a position on the same trading day. However, rather than getting out of the position quickly, you're going to be doing fewer trades and looking for a larger amount of profit per trade. This will give you some flexibility to trade with smaller lot sizes, but you will probably have to trade multiple lots at a time. While a scalper is probably going to do 10 or 20 trades per day, you're going to be looking for larger profits in the 3-10 trade per day range.

Position Trading

If you are a position trader, you are willing to hold a position for a very long time (in Forex terms). That means you will hold the position at least for weeks, and you are willing to hold it for months, or even more than a year. Think of position trading as longer-term swing trading. The techniques are going to be about the same, but you are willing to wait long term in order to take the kind of profits that you are looking for. Position traders are not people who frequently trade, and they may spend a long time on the sidelines waiting for the right time to enter a position.

News Traders

Items in the news, including political, economic, and trade news, can have a big impact on currency prices. The impact is probably not going to be very long-lived in most cases, but while it's working, it can cause big price moves. These days with the 24-hour news cycle, there are always new controversies coming up that are going to increase volatility and send the markets going one way or another. A news trader seeks to follow the news and enter trades when this happens, and then ride the wave of the trend that gets created from the result. For example, the president may remark (or issue a tweet) that would cause the U.S. dollar to either rise in value or fall by a large amount. As soon as the tweet was issued, the news trader would enter positions that they think are going to move a large amount as a result of the remark. So if the remark were one that would probably lead to a rise in the dollar against the Euro, the news trader would sell Euro/USD currency pairs. Then they would use the techniques of chart analysis to look for a reversal after the trend takes on momentum, and exit the trade when the trend shows signs of beginning to reverse.

Trend trading

Many traders simply trade with the trend, when a long-term trend one way or the other can be identified. This is also a technique that can be used in conjunction with swing trading or position trading. The trick is accurately identifying trends that appear to be set up for a long ride upward or downward. This is called trading with the trend, or some traders say the trend is your friend. If you are trend trading, you have the luxury of being able to trade less liquid currency pairs, provided that the trend is stable. Of course, no trend is going to be stable forever, but it should be stable enough, so that you can ride the trend for a long period to earn profits and then remain in the trend for a time, when you try and exit the position. If you are looking at currency pairs that are not as liquid, getting out of the position is not going to be as easy, but you should be able to do it while still making good profits. Trend trading works with any lot size, and you can do fewer numbers of trades and seek larger profits per trade.

End of Day Trading

If you are an end of day trader, you are taking a more relaxed approach to trading, looking at the markets at the end of your day, and doing your technical analysis to enter or exit trades. This type of trading can be used within the context of other trading styles like swing trading and position trading, but of course, it's not going to be used with scalping or intraday trading. People who will retain a full-time commitment and don't have time to follow the markets all day long may use end of day trading. End of day is a figurative phrase, since Forex markets are open 24 hours, so it's a time of day that you pick in order to do your trades. You can do your analysis at this time, and determine which trades to enter or exit. The low-key aspect of this trading style makes it suitable for all lot sizes, and it does require some patience. You will have more flexibility and be able to wait for the size of profits you are hoping to take, and so you don't necessarily have to enter a large number of trades.

CHAPTER 3:

Currencies Explained

The Major Currency Pairs

The U.S. Dollar is involved in some 89% of currency trades, and currency pairs that included the U.S. Dollar and some other currency from a large, developed economy are called the majors. There are seven major currency pairs. Let's take a look at each one so that you will be familiar with what people are talking about when they mention the majors. A significant currency pair can be any of the following.

EUR/USD

The Euro and U.S. Dollar currency pair is the most popular and widely traded of the majors. The Euro was introduced in 1999, and it's a relatively stable currency that represents all the major countries in Europe that are part of the European Union. Although Brexit is dominating recent headlines, even with Britain as a part of the European Union, it has maintained its currency, the Great British Pound. Hence, the Euro is the currency used by members of the EU on the continent.

When it comes to this currency pair, you are going to want to watch moves by the European Central Bank or ECB, and also the U.S. Federal Reserve. Of course, in any of the majors, you are going to be looking at moves by the U.S. Federal Reserve.

The biggest strength of this currency pair from the perspective of a small retail trader is that it is a highly liquid financial asset that often has substantial volatility. In recent years, the volatility and the magnitude of moves (on average) have decreased somewhat, but it's still a rather strong average pip movement of 200 pips. The currency pair is so liquid, getting in and out of trades fast is not going to be an issue. This currency pair is undoubtedly the right choice for beginners or a trader of any level.

USD/JPY

This is the U.S. Dollar and Japanese Yen currency pair. Japan isn't quite the monolith that it was in the 1980s when everyone thought that Japan would take over the entire world economically. However, Japan still maintains a large and powerful economy dominated by well-known companies like Toyota, Subaru, and Sony, among others. One factor that is important when considering this currency pair is the fact that Japan remains one of the world's largest exporting nations. This means that it's a frequently traded and highly liquid currency because all that exporting means that people have to convert dollars into Yens and vice versa all the time. The interest rate is low, which also makes this currency pair more attractive for holding over more extended periods.

GBP/USD

As we mentioned above, despite being a long-time member of the European Union, Great Britain held onto its currency rather than adopt the Euro in 1999. Now that Britain may exit the European Union, for good or for worse, this probably means that the Great British Pound is here to stay for the foreseeable future. We noted earlier in the book that this was once (and sometimes still is) referred to as the cable, as currency trading between the United States and Great Britain went on via electronic cable under the Atlantic Ocean starting in the late 19th century. Brexit may introduce a lot of volatility in this currency pair, and, in any currency pair involving GBP, and so traders may want to pay attention to it at least for the near future. Even after Brexit is finalized, if it ever actually is, then there is likely to be some extra volatility introduced into the price movements of GBP currency pairs. You are not favoring one currency over another because you like it, you are picking currencies based on what works in a given trade.

USD/CHF

CHF is the ticker symbol (to use a stock analogy) for the Swiss Franc. Switzerland is another country maintaining its currency, and given Switzerland's strong banking presence, it's a vital currency despite the relatively small size of the country and its economy. Traders consider the Swiss Franc to be an essential currency during times of economic trouble, or when there is an international crisis. When there are global problems, in most cases, the Swiss Franc can be expected to increase against the U.S. Dollar because the demand for the Franc rises as people look for a relatively safe place to put their money. So, if there is an economic crisis that you happen to experience, remember this and bet on the Swiss Franc against the Dollar. In times of uncertainty, economic downturn, or emergency, the Swiss Franc may also do well against several other currencies such as the Japanese Yen. The USD/CHF pair sometimes goes by the nickname "Swissie."

USD/CAD

Although Canada has a relatively small population compared to the European Union, Japan, and the United States, its economy enjoys outsized importance because it shares a border with the United States, and a large amount of trade goes on between the two countries. Canada has a lot of natural resources that it exports, such as oil, natural gas, and timber, which again helps it to maintain an outsized level of importance in the world of economics and currency trading. Due to its direct relationship with the United States, the USD/CAD currency pair can be a good trade, even though it doesn't play as significant a role in the markets as the EUR/USD currency pair does. When relations between Canada and the United States are good, volatility can decrease for this currency pair. When there are some difficulties, this can lead to increased volatility making it more attractive to trade. Canada has significant exports of coal, raw aluminum, iron ore, gold, and copper ore. So to get a feel for how the movement of the Canadian Dollar may be trending concerning other currencies, you might want to see if the prices of these commodities are rising or falling. Since Canada is exporting these materials, this generally means that rising commodity prices are good for Canadian currency.

AUD/USD

Australia is a diverse and highly modern economy, but like Canada, it's economic fortunes are often influenced very heavily by the export of natural resources. When it comes to Australia, you will want to pay attention to iron ore and rare earth metals, along with coal. When commodity prices are rising, the fortunes of Australia are often rising with it, but when they are declining, the wealth of Australia is probably going down as well. When you are trading any currency pair involving the Australian Dollar, you will want to look at the prices of various commodities. Still, especially coal and iron ore, to see how they are going. Australia also exports large amounts of gold, petroleum, and wheat. So favorable pricing moves for these commodities may put the Australian Dollar in a position to rise against other currencies.

NZD/USD

The last of the majors is the currency pair between the New Zealand Dollar and the U.S. Dollar. The New Zealand economy isn't as large as the others we've considered, and it's highly dependent on tourism and the export of agricultural products. It is a leading exporter of dairy products as well as lamb and other meats. If dairy prices are rising on commodities markets, this can bode well for any currency pair involving the NZD.

Crosses

If the USD is not in the currency pair, these are called crosses. There are crosses for each of the currencies from major economies, such as the Euro or the Japanese Yen. The majors enjoy the highest trading volume and are therefore the most liquid currency pairs that you can trade, but several crosses also have high trading volume, and so can be useful to trade as well.

First, let's look at some of the Euro crosses.

EUR/JPY: As you might imagine, there is a lot of trade that goes on between these two major economies. As a result, this can be a useful currency pair to trade. When exports are in favor, Japan might have an edge, in particular when electronic components are considered.

EUR/CHF: This is the Euro and Swiss Franc cross pair. The thing to look for here is the overall economic situation and whether there are any international tensions. Generally speaking, if people are looking for a safe refuge for their money, the Swiss Franc is going to be it. So when times are tough, you might look for increased volatility with this currency pair, and you might also look for the Swiss Franc to be rising in value against the Euro.

EUR/GBP: This is undoubtedly a currency pair to watch with the pending Brexit move, no matter how it turns out. If the situation is viewed favorably in terms of the European Union, then the Euro is going to rise in value against the Great British Pound. Shortly, at least, the Great British Pound is probably going to be declining in value against several major currencies, although over time, this will likely stabilize. Once things settle down, the Great British Pound is perhaps going to be rising in value. But for now, look for it to be the weaker member of a currency pair with another major country.

AUD: The Australian Dollar is also an excellent cross to look at when trading with the Japanese Yen, New Zealand Dollar, Euro, Canadian Dollar, and even against the Chinese Yuan. When commodity prices are rising, this is something that is going to favor the Australian Dollar against the currencies of those countries that are importing large amounts of raw materials from Australia. China is a significant consideration here.

Japanese Yen: Any cross pair involving JPY is going to be necessary. The essential data point for Japan is to remember that Japan has few (if any) natural resources. Still, it's going to be importing a large number of commodities since it has a thriving export business of primary manufactured goods like automobiles.

Exotic Currency Pairs

These are currencies that are not traded nearly as much, but many exotic currencies are going to be associated with developing countries. Examples can include countries like Mexico, Thailand, and Brazil. Some currencies that fall in the exotic category have manipulated or fixed exchange rates, making trading them problematic. The biggest weakness with exotic currencies is that they tend to have small trading volumes. Professional Forex traders are generally not spending their time focusing on exotic currency pairs.

Some exotics like the Mexican Peso are more stable than others, such as the Iraqi dinar. But the biggest weakness for any exotic currency is that traders do not highly desire them, and as a result, you might find yourself stuck in trade far longer than you want to be.

CHAPTER 4:

How To Concrete Start With Forex Trading With Practical Example – Step By Step

The first thing to get started besides educating yourself on how to trade is to open a trading or brokerage account. In many ways, this isn't too different from opening a stock trading account, and so it will be somewhat familiar to many readers. Some of the most leading brokerages also allow you to open a Forex trading account.

Step 1: Things to Look for When Selecting an FX Dealer

The first thing that I would consider if I were opening a new account is how experienced the dealer was. I would be less interested in opening an account with a brand-new dealer. The dealer may be legitimate, but you are taking a chance to open an account with someone who does not have a proven history. That was worth the gamble in the early days of Forex trading, but after 20 years, the market is in a more mature phase, and so there isn't any reason to be taking chances.

So, the first thing to consider is the length of time that the dealer has been in business. I would opt for at least five years of history, but you can shop around and find varying amounts of time in business. A longer time frame that the company has been in business means that the company is established and therefore is generally speaking, more trustworthy.

If a long time, the established brokerage has recently entered the Forex arena, that might be an exception. If the company is a well-known and experienced stock brokerage, then you know that this is a well-established and reliable business. They can be trusted to conduct honest trades, they are going to be upfront about their fees, and they are going to be trustworthy handling your financials.

Step 2: How to Open a Forex Trading Account

In some ways, opening a Forex trading account can be a little bit more complicated than opening a stock market account. The main reason is that Forex offers some opportunities for money laundering and other activities. As a result, a legitimate broker is going to be putting a little more effort into verifying your identity. Let's take a look at some of the steps involved in this process. Typically, when you open a stock trading account in your home country, all you have to do is link a bank account and provide some necessary information. When you open an account with an FX dealer, this is going to involve a few extra steps. It might take a little bit of time, but in the end, it will be no big deal. In a nutshell, legitimate FX dealers are required to verify that you are who you say you are and that you are a citizen and so forth. So what are the steps involved in the verification process?

The first is that you have to apply to open a trading account. This is a simple process that is done online. So, it will be familiar to anyone who has used for a credit card or anything else online. You will have to answer some simple questions about your identity, place of residence, and other necessary information. Then you are going to be required to provide documentation that the dealer uses to prove your identity to fight money laundering. You are going to have to prove that you are a citizen of the country, and you will also need to provide some proof of residence. In the United States, sending a copy of your driver's license is probably going to be adequate to verify your citizenship. I live in the United States so cannot give details on proving citizenship in other countries, please check with your local brokerage for more information.

Step 3: When Can You Begin Trading

Once the FX dealer has credited your account, you are ready to begin trading. This is done directly through the dealer's platform and often happens relatively quickly after you have initiated funding. You can trade 24 hours a day on business days. The beginning of the trading week starts in the late afternoon on Sunday, US Eastern time, when the markets in New Zealand open. These are going to be quickly followed by the market in Sydney, Australia, and Singapore, and then a little bit later, you will have Tokyo, Japan, and Hong Kong opening. London will be opening around 2 AM Eastern US time. You will be able to trade until the markets in New York close on Fridays, ending the trading week. So you have six days a week, 24 hours a day on most days to trade. This means that it's always active, and you can trade at hours that are the most convenient for your purposes.

Step 4: Some Well-Known FX dealers

In this section, we will take a look at a few of the well-known FX dealers that operate inside the United States. Some of them are also stock brokerages. I have to be honest that while there are many good options, I tend to favor the stock brokerages because these are dependable companies that have been around for a long time. Also, if you are also trading stocks or options, it can save you a little bit of hassle, since you can have one brokerage to handle everything that you are doing. That said, some people like to keep their Forex activities separate from other trading activities. The way you set this up is entirely personal, and so there are no rules to follow, other than selecting a well-respected and legitimate dealer.

Forex dealers are regulated in the United States. This is done by the National Futures Association, and also by the Commodity Futures Trading Commission. The regulation of these dealers helps to ensure that there are some protections in place for individual traders. Not to pick on the Bahamas, and I am sure many legitimate companies are operating in the Bahamas. Still, when you put your money in an overseas outfit that is not as tightly regulated, you put yourself at risk for being victimized, loss of capital, and lack of the kinds of protections that you get in the United States.

Step 5: Spreads

We will discuss spreads, but this is the way that brokerage dealers charge commissions on Forex. So when looking for a reputable dealer, you are also going to be wanting to take a look at the spreads they charge and compare them in between your options.

No matter what happens, as long as you have selected the right brokerage, this should not be too much of an issue.

CHAPTER 5:

How To Trade Without Emotions

With a correct attitude towards forex trading, you can be sure to achieve your goals. Here are a few suggestions that can help you develop the proper manner and mindset for forex trading and trading in general.

Be Patient

This is a virtue when it comes to forex trading, as it helps one cover everything at the right time and with the right state of mind. Patience can get you out of trouble as sometimes you might be forced to enter into a market hastily without understanding how it works. For beginners, Patience is a crucial aspect as you get to understand the pros and cons of forex trading. Patience also keeps you away from reacting out of a bad day in business and even making wrong choices and decisions that can cause significant losses. As the adage goes, Patience pays, so take your time off a hectic day and trust the process.

Be Objective

In forex trading, one is required to be objective and not trade with emotions. As stated earlier, a forex trader should keep the eyes on the final product, that is, his financial goals. Being subjective or acting on emotions is disastrous for any business, and learning to work by the book is key to a successful forex trading career. This means that you should not also listen to people who claim to be Pros in the game and trust your trading patterns instead of sheepishly following the crowd. This doesn't, however, mean that you should not trade on mass thinking, but if you do, always keep in mind that the masses are not still right.

Be Disciplined

This ought to be a significant aspect in every business, and as earlier pointed out, discipline keeps one out of overreacting for a loss or a win. This cuts across happy and sad moments in business as both sides can affect the outcome if not subjected to some discipline. Being able to control yourself, to not overtrade or under trade, and take just enough risks is a skill that can be learned by following procedures and sticking to the game-plan. Remember, you should never, ever, stake half your capital, risk all your profits or worse, trade with money you don't have or money you can't afford to lose.

Be Realistic

Just like any other business, one should be real and expect a particular profit according to the capital traded-in. Always remember that forex trading is not like Lotto or betting where one can win a jackpot of a million dollars by stalking just a little money. It takes time to build up your skills, your knowledge, and your confidence and secure good profits with forex trading. Therefore, one should expect the right amount of returns on investment and what comes with it. By not giving up, being disciplined and patient, and doing your research, you might end up achieving your goals and reaching top-level in the forex world. This mentality helps one to limit the number and types of transactions on a daily or weekly basis and to stay in the game even after losing a small percentage of the initial investment. This is a business opportunity, just like any other.

There are rules to abide by to reach your potential and, most importantly, realize your potential in terms of profit. Below are 12 rules that can help you achieve your goals in Forex Trading.

1 Trust the Process

Forex trading is a business and needs time and effort to grow and consolidate, which means that there is more than just waiting for profits. Profit oriented businesses can end if the thresholds one has set are not met, and the overall approach is not thoroughly planned. Any business is not only buying and selling as it involves huddles and logistics to make the whole institution work and doable. Some profit-oriented forex traders tend to give up easily if they don't meet their target after a few operations or a short period. However, one can set a timeline and work towards meeting the set target without having to achieve a specific point, which might turn to be the opposite. some points are process-oriented and help in reaching the high note in forex trading and are outlined.

2 Outline Daily Activities

Day to day activities can only be achieved when put down on paper for a specific task in forex trading. Having in mind the right thing to do on a specific day is good as it helps to avoid distractions and other things that may get in the way on a business day. This means that the more you know what you are doing on a busy day, you will not waste time doing other things that do not help achieve your goal and the needs you want to build your forex trading skills.

3 Analyze the Market

As pointed out earlier, trading with emotions is bad for business as it does not go by the plans and strategy, but with the reaction of business gone wrong or even a big win. Being greedy is so bad in forex trading, and it is advisable to analyze the market first before trying out forex trading and giving a shot on the most promising patterns. When you play by the rules, you train the mind to follow the right procedures and even helps in becoming more discipline in forex trading. Training the mind helps in a vulnerable situation, which will make you hold on when there is a crisis.

4 Be Defensive

This is another important rule to follow in forex trading, for it is the core purpose of joining the business and what will keep you survive storms that will come your way in one way or the other. This simply means that you should not trade everything, including your capital, defend your initial capital, and aim at making profits. When you make a target and do not meet it, then at least you tried, but trading profusely just to meet the target with limited time is not good at all, as it is an offensive approach. You should always protect your capital as it is the only thing keeping you in the business, and one mistake can send you to factory reset, i.e., going back to the drawing board wondering when the rain started beating you.

5 Have A Trading Plan

Just like any other venture, Forex trading needs a business plan that has been tested to be working and giving impressive results. The plan involves things that you need to do from A-Z; this may include the rules of engagement, trading pattern, market analysis, and other key aspects that make the business run well. After making the trading plan, you can test it virtually to see if it will go well with the market and if it is good, then give it the green light and start the forex trading. But make sure that you outline the plan as it is the backbone of the whole venture.

6 Know That Trading Is A Business

Forex trading is like a business and should be treated as such for one to get the best out of it by giving the attention it deserves. Other researches have talked about not comparing trading with job opportunities or hobby to be done in leisure time. This means that one should not expect a salary and works on getting profits and paying attention and not only focusing on it when you are free. With this, a forex trader will learn to prioritize forex trading just like any other business.

7 Outline Risk

Make sure that you point out the risk you intend to get yourself into and do not give it too much until you are out of business. Do not risk an amount that you cannot afford; risking is only for the amount you are capable of and not anywhere near initial capital. Remember, as said earlier, if you lose capital, that means that you are out of business, and you will not want that to happen to you. Only risk an amount that you know if they go, then you will not struggle with bringing back the business into living.

8 Use Technology

The modern era of inventions and innovations can be a plus in forex trading as it helps improve the outcome of a venture. Technology has played a big role in forex trading, thanks to innovators who come with new things every day to enhance the world in bringing people closer. With technology, one can trade anywhere in the world monitor charts using a computer or even mobile phones. This means that one can travel all over the world as well as working at the same time. This has been evident for bloggers and travel entrepreneurs who blog for a living and promote products online while they travel. This can be the same for forex traders, and it helps in even having a good time and relaxing the mind while working.

9 Have A Stop Loss

This is somehow similar to outlining risk but specifies the amount that one should be willing to lose in particular trading.

In Forex trading, you should only lose what you afford, and it is essential to outline the amount or percentage that one should only lose in trading. This also acts as a disciplined mode as it helps in controlling the mind and emotions not to surpass the limited amount of possible risk.

10 Focus on The Bigger Picture

What is the purpose of starting forex trading? Can you do the business to be aligned in that direction? Are you getting some profits and losing sometimes? then you are on the right track heading to greatness in forex trading.

Business is not about just making profits but making impacts on a personal level and getting more skills. So what is your bigger picture? To have gained at least 10 percent in the financial year 2020-2021? Having this in mind, then you can be sure of aiming in the right way as compared to only focusing on maximizing profits.

11 Keep Learning Markets

Forex trading is an ongoing process even after mastering markets and getting out of an amateur venture. One does not stop learning at anything, and things keep changing in the forex world; this is important to keep an open mind in everything to do with business. Some of the skilled forex traders can fall prey to crowd psychology, and some markets are unpredictable, making forex trading a learning experience every time one is trading.

12 Be A Progressive Trader

Every forex trader wants to earn profit as it is the main reason for venturing in forex trading in the first place, but are you only profit-oriented the first day in the market, or are you moving forward? Learning also can be huge progress as it helps one avoid making similar mistakes and open ways for more profit in the future. A progressive trade is the one that celebrates every win, either small or big, as long as it is a victory. Just like a child, you learn to sit then start crawling and in no time you start taking a few steps and eventually running. The same applies to forex trading, you gradually move from one stage to the other, and you cannot jump directly to only making profits. You either win or learn. After making a trading plan and testing it, one can join the trading business and encounter ups and downs as it shapes the ultimate goal of forex trading. With this progress, one can be sure of securing a future in forex trading full of experiences and lots of encounters that can prepare you for any hard hurdles that one might come across during your trading experience.

CHAPTER 6:

How To "Win" Forex Market and Create Passive Income – Step By Step Guide

Making Passive Income in The Forex Market

We do two things in the forex market; we either peddle or acquiring currencies. It is easy to place trades in the market and works similarly to that of the stock market. Anyone with experience in the stock market can perform trade actions in the forex.

Understanding Forex Quotes

When buying a particular currency, the exchange rate tells you the amount to compensate in terms of the quote currency to purchase an entity of the base currency. For instance, in our illustration, you have to wage 1.51258 for you to buy a single British pound

However, if you were to sell, you will get 1.51258 U.S. dollars for each 1 British pound you sell. The basis for buying or selling is the "base currency." You should not forget this because, without this understanding, your knowledge of forex will be distorted. This means that if you want to buy GBP/USD, it implies you are purchasing the base currency while trading the quote currency simultaneously. In a nonprofessional language, you buy GBP while selling USD.

If you anticipate the base currency to acknowledge proportionate to the quote currency, then you have to buy the currency. However, if you expect depreciation in the base currency, then the best option is to sell.

Determining to Buy Or Sell

Before going further, you have to establish to buy or sell a particular currency. Remember, buying and selling are not the same. A simple way to differentiate them is as follows:

Buying factors, you are acquiring the base currency while trading the quote currency. This connotes that you want a rise in the value of the base currency and peddle it back at a higher price. In forex, we use terminology such as taking a "long position" or "going long. To make it easier long is equivalent to buy

Bid and Ask Price

Now you know the difference between buying and selling the base currency in forex, it is essential to talk about the bid and ask price. Do not be confused when you see currency pairs quoted at two different rates. This indicates the proposal and asks the price, and in a better situation, the bid price is always lower in comparison to the asking price.

The bid price is the price your intermediary decides to purchase the base currency against the quote currency. It is the best price convenient at that time at which the trader is inclined to sell. Alternatively, the asking price is that a broker is willing to sell the base currency in exchange for the quote currency.

Time to Make Money

I know you are fired up to understand how to make money in the market. Well, in the examples below, I will teach you how you can use essential analysis to select to either buy or sell a particular currency pair. If you did economics while in school, then this section will be attractive to you. Notwithstanding, just act like you know everything I am going to talk about. Even if you do not understand, do not worry because the light is at the end of the tunnel, and you will surely reach there.

EUR/USD Pair

By now, I am convinced you now know the base and quote currency. Well, the euro is our base currency in this example and the basis for which we buy/sell. This is how traders make a profit – when they anticipate that the U.S. economy will fall, which is terrible news for the dollars; they will trigger a buy option of the EUR/USD pair. By doing so, the trader has purchased the euros in anticipation that it will rise against the U.S. dollar.

Alternatively, if the trader believes the U.S. economy will is strong. In contrast, the euro will fall adjacent to the dollar, and he will trigger the sell option, which allows him to sell the euros in anticipation that the price will fall.

USD/JPY

Always remember, the base currency is on the left while the quote currency is on the right-hand side. Our base currency, in this example, is the U.S. dollar and is the basis for our buy/sell. You will execute a buy option if you think the Japanese government will weaken its currency to boost its export industry. By this option, you have purchased the U.S. dollar in anticipation that the dollar will rise against the Yen.

However, if your hunch tells you that Japanese investors will pull their money from the U.S. financial market and exchange their dollars to yen, this will affect the U.S. dollar, and the best option is to execute the sell order. In this situation, you have sold the dollar while anticipating that it will depreciate when compared with the Japanese yen.

USD/CHF

This will be the last example of this session. The base currency is the U.S. dollar. If, as a trader, you consider the CHF overvalued, then you can trigger the buy order. In doing so, you have anticipated that the dollar will inflate over the Swiss Franc. However, if you consider the opposite, then you could execute the sell order. This means you anticipate a depreciation in the value of the U.S. dollar over the Swiss Franc.

Pips and Pipettes

A pip is the unit of measurement to represent a change in terms of value that exists between two different currencies. Let us assume the following pair GBP/USD moves from 1.3250 to 1.3251. In this situation, the currency moves a pip. You will observe that the pip is the last decimal place of a particular pair. It is usually the fourth decimal place of any currency. However, if such a couple contains the Yen, then it is two decimal places.

For example, the pair GBP/USD moves from 1.35421 to 1.35422, and it has driven a single pipette. Because every currency has its unique value, it is essential to evaluate the cost of a pip for each currency.

The examples below we are using quotes that have four decimal places. In the cases below, the USD is the base currency.

USD/CAD at 1.5890

To get the pip value, that will be

Pip value = 0.0001/exchange rate

Therefore, in our example, that will be 0.0001/1.5890, which is equivalent to 0.00006293.

USD/CHF at 1.4898

Pip values = 0.0001/1.4898

=0.00006712

USD/JPY at 118.45

Did you notice anything different? Of course, the quote currency has two decimal points, whereas most currencies have four decimal places. In this situation, a single pip movement will be .01, which will be divided by the exchange rate to get the value of the pip. Therefore, that will be:

.01/118.45

Pip value =0.0008442

In the examples above, the USD is the base currency. In the following examples, I will explain situations where the USD is not quoted first.

EUR/USD at 1.2120

Pip value = 0.0001 divided by exchange rate

0.0001/1.2120

EUR value = 0.00008250

However, we do not have to stop at the EUR; we have to go back to the U.S. dollar. To do that, it will be EUR x exchange rate.

0.00008250 x 1.2120

Rounding up the value, that will be 0.00001

I believe you understood what we did here because of the following examples; I will do the calculation without any explanation.

AUD/USD at 0.6752

.0001/0.6752

AUD = 0.0001418

To get the USD = 0.0001418*0.6752

=0.0001

Well, you do not have to border yourself with the calculations because your forex broker will help you sort this out. However, it is important to understand how your broker arrives at those figures. You can save yourself the stress if your broker does not do the calculation by using an online pip value calculator.

What is a lot?

We trade spot forex in specific amounts known as lots. We have mini, micro, and Nano lot sizes in the forex. However, the ideal lot size is 100,000 units.

Lot Size	Lot Unit
Nano	100
Micro	1,000
Mini	10,000
Standard	100,000

You have to trade a large amount of a currency pair to see any consequential loss or profit while trading. In the following example, I am using a standard lot size, which is equivalent to a 100,000 unit. The calculation will show how the pip value is affected.

USD/JPY at 118.45 = (0.1/118.45)*100,000 = $8.44 per pip

GBP/USD at 1.7030 = (0.0001/1.7030)*100,000 = $5.87 per pip

EUR/USD at 1.2500 = (0.0001/1.2500)*100000 = $8 per pip

What Is Leverage?

Remember, in the beginning, when I told you how you could use a small amount to trade big. Yes, that is what call leverage in forex. You can consider your forex broker as a bank, who gives you upfront investment funds of $100,000 to trade in the market. All the bank is asking is for you to come up with a thousand dollars. In other words, a deposit of $1,000 gives you $100,000 to trade in the market. Does that sound too correct for such hard times? Well, that is what leverage is when we talk about forex.

Notwithstanding, the total leverage you can on your forex broker. Usually, your broker will request a trade deposit, which is also the "initial margin" or "account margin." Immediately after the deposit, you can start trading currencies.

Market Order in Forex

A market order is simply an order placed by the trader to either sell or buy a currency pair at the best price available. For instance, let us assume that the bid price for USD/CAD presently stood at 1.3450, whereas the asking price is 1.3453. If you intended to buy USD/CAD at the market, then the seller will sell it to you using the asking price of 1.3453. Then you have to execute the buy option to purchase it at that price.

Types of Orders

This is similar to what major eCommerce stores do. You saw a beautiful pair of shoes and checked the price, you are satisfied with it, and you clicked the buy option, which indicates the current amount of the shoe. Notwithstanding, in the foreign exchange market, you either sell or buy currencies pairs. Nevertheless, in the eCommerce stores, you have the option of only buying things.

Limit Entry Order

This particular market order is placed when the buyer wants to sell above or buy below the market at a specific price. Let us assume USD/CAD is currently trading at 1.1290, and your objective is to go short peradventure the price gets to the 1.1300 marks. You are faced with two options. To sit and watch your trade for it to hit your target or you place a sell limit order at the targeted price (1.1300).

I will tell you the disadvantage of the first one; you have to abandon everything you are doing to wait for it to reach your target. Are you going to sit with your monitor for hours? Well, with a sell limit order, you can shut your computer and work on other projects. Once the price reaches the 1.1300 marks, the trading platform you are using will automatically perform the sell order using the best price available.

When to use this order, type is when you anticipate a price reversal once it got to the price you detailed.

Stop-Entry Order

This order is required when you want to place a trade to buy above or sell below the current market. This is usually at a specific price, which must be indicated in the trading platform. For instance, EUR/USD is currently trading at 1.9080 and is moving in an upward direction. You anticipate the price will go higher in that direction if it gets to the 1.9090 mark. I know you will not want to sit in front of your computer pending when the price reaches the 1.9090 mark. However, with the stop-entry order, the platform will automatically close the trade once it gets to that point.

CHAPTER 7:

Money Mistake to Avoid

Now we'll turn our attention to giving some tips, tricks, and advice on errors to avoid ensuring as much as possible that you have a successful time trading.

Avoid the Get Rich Quick Mentality

Any time that people get involved with trading or investing, the hope is always there that there's a possibility of the big winning trade. It does happen now and then. But quite frankly, it's a rare event. On many occasions, even experienced traders are guessing wrong and taking losses. It's essential to approach Forex for what it is. It's a business. It is not a gambling casino even though a lot of people treated that way, so you need to come to your Forex business—and it is a business no matter if you do it part-time or quit your job and devote your entire life to it—with the utmost seriousness. You wouldn't open a restaurant and recklessly buy 1 thousand pounds of lobster without seeing if customers were coming first. So, why would you approach Forex as if you were playing slots at the casino? Take it seriously and act as if it's a business because it is.

Trade Small

You should always trade small and set small achievable goals for your trading. The first benefit of purchasing small is that this approach will help you avoid a margin call. Second, it will also help you set profit goals that are small and achievable. That will help you stay in business longer.

Simply put, you will start gaining confidence and learning how to trade if you get some trades that make $50 profits, rather than shooting for a couple of deals that would create thousands of dollars in one shot, but and up making you broke. Again, treat your trading like a real business. If you were opening a business, chances are you would start looking for slow and steady improvements, and you certainly would not hope to get rich quick.

Let's get specific. You are trading small means, never trading standard lots. Even if you have enough cash to open an account such that you could trade standard lots, I highly recommend that you stay away from them. A large amount of capital involved and margin that would be used could just get you into a lot of financial trouble.

Be Careful With Leverage

It's incredibly beneficial. It allows you to enter and trades that would otherwise not be possible. On the other hand, the temptation is there to use all your leverage in the hopes of making it big on one or two trades. You need to avoid using up all your advantage. Remember that you can have a margin call and get yourself into big trouble if your trades go wrong. And it's important to remember there's a high probability that some of your trades are going to go wrong no matter how carefully you do all your analysis.

Not Using A Demo Account

A big mistake the beginners make is jumping in too quickly. There is a reason that most broker-dealers provide demos or simulated accounts. If you don't have a clue what that reason is, let's go ahead and stated here. Brokers offer demo accounts because Forex is a high-risk trading activity. It can be something that offers a lot of rewards, and it does for large numbers of traders. But there is a substantial risk of losing your capital. Many beginners are impatient, hoping to make money right away. That's certainly understandable, but you don't want to fall into that trap. Take 30 days to practice with a demo account. This will provide several advantages. Trading on Forex is different than trading on the stock market. Using the demo account, you can become familiar with all the nuances of Forex trading. This includes everything from studying the charts, to placing your orders and, most importantly, understanding both pips and margin. The fact that there is so much leverage available means you need to learn how to use it responsibly.

Failing To Check Multiple Indicators

There is also a temptation to get into trades quickly just on a gut level hunch. You need to avoid this approach at all costs. Some beginners will start learning about candlesticks, and then when they first start trading, they will recognize a pattern on a chart. Later amid the excitement, they will enter a large trade based on what they saw. And then they will end up on the losing end of a trade. Some people are even worse, and they don't also look at the candlesticks. Instead, they just look at the trend and think they better get in on it, and they got all anxious about doing so. That means first checking the candlesticks and then confirming at least with the moving average before entering or exiting a position. You should also have the RSI handy, and you may or may not want to use Bollinger bands.

Use Stop Loss and Take Profit Orders

Well, I hate to repeat myself yet again, but this point is significant. I am emphasizing it over and over because it's one of the tools that you can use to protect yourself from heavy losses. One of the ways that you can get out of having to worry about margin calls and running out of money is to put stop-loss orders every time you trade. This will require studying the charts more carefully. You need to have an obvious idea where you want to get out of the trade if it doesn't go in the direction you hoped. But if you have a stop-loss order in place, then you can avoid the problem of having your account just go down the toilet. Secondly, although the temptation is always there to look for as many profits as possible, in most cases, you should opt to set a take profit order when you make your trade.

Remember Price Changes Are In Pips

Beginners often make the mistake of forgetting about pips. If you have trouble with pips and converting them to actual money, go back and review the examples we provided. Remember that pips play a central role in price changes; you need to know your dollar value per pip to keep tabs on your profit and losses. This is also important for understanding the right stop loss and take profit orders to execute.

Don't Try Too Many Strategies or Trading Styles At Once

When you are a beginning Forex trader, it can be tempting to try everything under the sun. That can be too much for a lot of people. The most advisable thing to do is to stick with one strategy, so don't try scalping and being a position trader at the same time. The shorter the time frame for your trades, the more time and energy you have to put into each trade. Scalping and day trading are activities that would require full-time devotion. They are also high-pressure, and that can help enhance emotions involved in the trades. For that reason, I don't recommend those styles or strategies for beginners. In my opinion, and to be honest, it's mine alone, I think position trading is also too much for a beginner. It requires too much patience.

Perhaps the best strategy to use when you're beginning Forex trading is to become a swing trader. It's an excellent middle ground between the most extremely active trading styles and something that is going to try people's patience, such as position trading. When you do swing trading, you can do periods more extended than a day indeed, but as long or short as you need to meet your goals otherwise.

Market Expectations

Life as a forex trader can sometimes get lonely. After all, this is the kind of career where you are entirely on your own. You enjoy your profits alone, but you also suffer losses on your own. There is no one in the forex market whom you can depend on to comfort you.

Therefore, it is also useful if you connect with like-minded people. Feel free to make friends with other traders. After all, you are all players in the market who want the same thing. The good thing is that you are not competing with one another. You can even help one another by sharing information, insights, and strategies.

Have Fun

Forex trading is fun. This is a fact. Many traders get to enjoy this kind of life that they continue to learn despite their losses. It is also not uncommon to find traders, especially beginners, who spend their whole day just learning about forex trading. Like gambling in a casino, trading currencies can also be very addicting, especially if you are making a nice profit from it.

Learn to have fun and enjoy the journey. Sometimes taking things too seriously can ruin the experience and even make you less productive. In your life as a trader, you will make some mistakes from time to time. You would experience losing money from what otherwise would have been a profitable trade if only you knew better. Do not get too stressed. The important thing is for you to learn as much as you can from every mistake. Take it easy, but remember to learn from the experience. Making mistakes is part of the learning process. Of course, you should try to minimize them as much as possible. Learn and have fun.

CHAPTER 8:

Personal Recommendation

Tips For Success

Take advantage of volatility: Over time, the general baseline of the forex market has only grown more volatile. This means that if you want to compete in the forex market successfully, you are going to need to use this fact to your advantage. Generally speaking, there are two types of volatility that you will need to keep an eye out for, implied volatility and historical volatility. Historical fluctuations will help you determine how a specific currency has acted over a set period while implied volatility measures the current level of volatility a currency has at the moment and what it is more likely to look like in the future.

Diversify: While you will want to stick to a few different currency pairs when you are first getting started in the forex market, over time, you are going to want to diversify to find real success. Not only will this make it possible for you to ensure that a single wrong turn won't wipe out your trading capital, but it will also ensure that there is always something to focus on when your favored currency pairs aren't giving you much to work.

Never forget that, regardless of how thorough your research is, you can never trust a specific trade to go your way completely, especially if the market is currently in the midst of a period of high volatility. Spreading your trading capital around will thus provide you with a way to somewhat standardize profits, even in the middle of the unexpected. If trading in the forex market were gambling, then diversifying your holdings would be hedging your bets.

In this instance, a significant player is any entity that is massive enough to ensure that their trades are enough to cause ripples throughout the market as a whole.

One of the most commonly watched major players is national banks. Necessarily, they are the ones who set the bid price because they are the ones buying up currency most frequently. Even better, they often telegraph their moves to a significant degree, which means you can often learn what their movements are going to be if you take the time to look for them.

Read more economic reports: For every frequently traded currency, there are likely to be dozens, if not hundreds of relevant financial statements released each year.

This means that you are going to want to always be up to date on the latest economic reports on the currency pairs you favor as well as keeping an actively updated calendar with any relevant dates well-marked. If these early reports become widespread enough, they can even start their trends as they push the market in one direction or another.

Don't stick with your first broker or dealer forever: When getting started in forex, it makes sense to pick a cheap broker who doesn't require all that much trading capital to be present and accounted for before you start trading. There are far more relevant concerns for a more experienced trader to consider, which means that once you have a firm grasp of the basics, you are going to want to reevaluate your choice and look into brokers or dealers that offer more competitive benefits.

While many forex dealers refer to themselves brokers or brokerages, the difference between the two can generally be summed up in whether the company you are working with is willing to trading with or against you (dealer) or if they are setting up trades against other amiable parties (broker). Brokerages also often offer training courses and other extras that may appeal to new traders, while dealers usually provide a more bare-bones experience.

While many new traders will benefit from the oversight that a broker brings to the process, as you gain more experience, you may find that the flexibility and lower cost of a dealer make them a natural choice for your purposes. You are going to want to focus on more than which dealer has the lowest fees; however, as oversight is essential. After all, if you choose a dealer who has no official control, then you will mostly have no recourse if they end up taking your money and then disappearing.

Practice your patience: Another crucial part of money management when it comes to trading in the forex market is patience. While it is easy for new traders to feel the need to be continually trading, the fact of the matter is that there are always going to be times when the best option is to sit things out for a little while until your possibilities improve. This will come along with an understanding that the market is prone to moving in a wide variety of ways, only a few are going to result in the types of trends that are well defined enough to make it worth to at least attempt to make a profit from it.

Avoid anger and fear: When it comes to emotions that cloud your mind and kill your successful trade percentage, there is nothing less productive to active trading than rage. Anger is an insidious problem as it can often cloud your judgment slowly over time, making it difficult to see what is happening until it is too late. Rather than letting your anger influence the decision-making process, you will instead need to focus on keeping your losses to a minimum by working quickly to expel any angry feelings before they start to affect your successful trade percentage.

Besides anger, the emotion that you are going to need to deal with most frequently are going to fear. Whether it is the fear of missing out or the fear of committing to a trade, if you start listening to fear rather than the facts that you have available to you, your trading capital will suffer. While it is perfectly natural to be a little fearful when it comes to making significant trades, especially if they have the potential for high risk and great rewards, if you let it take over, then you will never reach your full potential.

There are two primary ways of getting over your fear, the first of which is by never starting a trade that you can't afford to lose. Investing is never a sure thing, which is why the potential for profit is so great, and the sooner you learn to live with that fact, the better. The only other way to mitigate fear is with practice. Remember, the more you trade, the more comfortable the entire process will feel.

CHAPTER 9:

Risk and Money Management

This focuses on how to budget for profit when trading forex and expounds on how you can manage risk and use leverage to your advantage. Addresses how the timeframe affects operations in forex.

Budgeting for Profit

Budgeting for profit means that you have to understand how the forex market works.

If you want to make profits when forex trading, there are a few tips you can use. For instance, ensure that you start small. This advice applies mainly to those who are new to forex trading; you can only be successful at trading millions when you have learned how to handle a few dollars as you can be successful in trading dollars when you have learned how to trade pennies. If you are lucky enough to buy many small stocks, there is a probability that they could tremendously increase in value, earning you profits. Luckily, there are traders today who can allow you to open an account with just a few dollars. If you constantly use the account, over time, your profits will begin to grow, and you will begin to experience success.

Additionally, if you want to succeed, you should be a regular investor. This does not mean you have to put in huge chunks of money for trading each time. It simply means that you could add manageable amounts to your investment every week — for instance, $10 or $20 per week. Being a regular investor not only refines your craft but also grows a sizeable account when the profits are compounded over time.

When you invest small amounts, you will not feel the pinch, but the rewards will be great regardless.

Another tip when budgeting for profit is to be patient. As has been highlighted above, starting small is a good move. However, many people get frustrated because of the slow process. To enhance your tolerance, trade small, but do not view these small amounts as dollars. Instead, view them as percentages. If you get a profit of, let us say $1 when you have a $10 dollar account, then you have made a 10% profit.

On the other hand, if you lose a dollar, then you have lost 10%. You will then have learned a valuable lesson about forex trading at a low cost of just a dollar. Also, when you trade in bits, you learn to deal with the hurdles associated with learning how to trade forex.

Risk management

Risk management involves reducing the size of potential losses while getting the most benefit out of a single trade. Risk management is highly debated as a topic in forex trading and, yet, it remains important as an aspect of trading because of the volatile nature of the forex market. To understand risk management in detail, read on.

One of the fundamental rules of managing risk when trading forex is to ensure that you only risk what you can afford to lose. Interestingly, many traders make the mistake of investing more than they can afford to lose, especially when they are learning the trade. As a forex trader, however, you can avoid some of the fundamental mistakes made by traders and become an outstanding trader yourself. You should know when to cut your losses. Cutting of losses can be done in two ways. The first is when you impose a mental stop and decide that the right thing to do would be to limit the drawdown, you can take on a trade. Another way through which you can control losses is by using a trading platform that has technology that allows you to lock in stops when your losses reach a particular level.

To control risks, you can also use the correct lot sizes. When brokers advertise accounts, they make it seem like a good idea to open an account with, let us say, $300 and use leverage to enhance mini-lot trades. They make it look like this technique will help double your money in just a single trade. This kind of thinking can sometimes deviate so far from the reality. When starting as a new trader, it is important to start small so that you have many options for managing the trade.

Another risk management strategy that you can employ in your trading is to understand the nature of the currency pairs you have decided to trade. Understand the events scheduled to take place in the day and even week ahead and how the data looks. Look at your trade plan's time horizon and consider liquidity conditions. Have a clear view of what the market has priced in and out because anticipating market events can alert you of the possible disruptive circumstances even if it is not a complete indicator of how you can win a trade. By understanding that risk varies across currency pairs, based on different factors such as liquidity, data sensitivity, and volatility, you will be better placed at understanding the analytical tools and strategies that are best for you.

Also, you can trade with an edge. This means that you do not have to be in the market all the time despite the fact that the currency market operates round the clock. Block the noise and do not let it pull you in. You can do this, for instance, by picking a spot and timing yourself. Also, look for setups in which there is a clear risk/reward scenario to avoid an unnecessary headache. Being an opportunist in the real world can be a problem, but that does not mean this strategy cannot work in the digital world of forex trading. You can take your time looking at the coming trade opportunities and use these chances instead of getting caught up in the market moves of a single moment.

Look forward to future opportunities because there will be more opportunities and it pays to be ready.

It is also important that as a trader, you take your profits regularly. When you take your profits, you are, in essence, reducing your exposure to risks in the market. You may find that your trade plan has an aggressive profit target but imagine what would happen if events do not play in your favor. It is, therefore, a better idea to protect what you have already worked for instead. After all, nobody has ever gone broke while taking profit. This is a tactic that can be referred to as taking money off the table. If you keep your profits in your margin account, you are likely to be subject to future trading decisions and are susceptible to unknown risks. Taking money out of your account keeps you in a position where you can trade in comfortable sizes. As you trade, remember that trading is not purely a game of profits, you can as well use the profits you make to do other things. You can invest the profits into another venture once you withdraw them. Additionally, you should ensure accuracy by double-checking. By now, you must have understood that currency trading takes place in a fairly fast-paced environment. It is even faster, thanks to electronic trading. There is, therefore, a risk in human error when inputting orders and trades, and this may have serious implications for you as a trader. For instance, what would be the benefit of putting in place a stop-loss order if it not entered for the right amount of currency? As a result, it would pay to make it a part of your routine to double-check your order and trade entries to avoid unnecessary mistakes that may prove costly to your forex trading venture. Ideally, it would be good to double-check figures immediately you input them and just before submission. Mistakes happen, but this does not mean you let minor errors become the source of your downfall.

Leverage

By now, you must have an idea of what leverage is and what it can do for you in forex trading.

In forex, leverage can be described as the ratio of the trader's funds that you are allowed to use to the size of the broker's available funds. In essence, leverage is whatever capital you borrow to increase your returns potentially. In reality, the leverage size usually exceeds invested capital to a large extent. Leverage is not fixed in all companies and may largely depend on the trading conditions provided by the forex brokers. Using leverage can sometimes be a risky affair because just like a double-edged sword, it may work to your favor or not. Below, we highlight how leverage works and how it can affect your bottom-line.

How leverage works

When you take leverage, it essentially means that you have borrowed from a broker. To calculate the margin-based average, you should divide your total transaction value by the amount of margin required.

The formula is thus:

Margin-Based Leverage = Total Value of Transaction / Margin Required

If therefore, you are required to top up 2% of the transaction's total value as margin, and you intend to trade a standard lot of USD/CHF equivalent to $200,000, the required margin would be 4,000 dollars. The margin-based leverage, in this case, would be 200,000/4,000, which equates to 50:1.

Interestingly, margin-based leverage does not affect risk. Whether a trader is required to top up a percentage of the transaction, therefore, does not influence the profits and losses they make. An investor always has the chance to attribute more than the required margin when trading. Real leverages rather than margin-based leverages have a stronger influence on profit and loss.

Calculating the real average would require you to divide the total face value of open positions by the capital you have for trading. As such:

Real Leverage = Total Value of Transaction / Total Trading Capital

For instance, let us say you have $20,000 in your our account and the position you open is worth $200,000 (one lot). Your leverage will be 200,000/20,000. If you traded two lots with the same amount in your account, then the leverage on your account would be 400,000/20,000, which is 20 times.

The margin-based leverage is, therefore, equal to the real leverage you can use to trade. Most traders, however, do not make use of their entire accounts as margin, and this is why their real and margin-based leverages tend to differ. It is generally advised that you do not use all your available margin. You should only use your leverage if you clearly have an advantage on your side.

You should first establish the extent of risk in terms of pips numbers so that you determine the potential capital loss you are likely to incur. The general rule states that the loss should be less than 3% of your capital, if you leverage a position and the potential loss comes to approximately 30% of the capital, then you should reduce your leverage by an equal 30%. As an experienced trader, you may deviate from the standard 3%.

You may also calculate the margin level that you should use, to determine the level of risk a trade poses. Let us say you have $10,000 in your account and you decide that you are trading ten mini USD/JPY lots. A move in one pip in a mini account is around a dollar, but when trading minis, the amount rises to approximately $10 each. If you trade 100 minis, then a pip move will be worth approximately $100. If therefore, you take a stop-loss of 30 pips, you have a representation of a potential $30 in a mini lot and $3,000 for 100 mini lots. With $10,000, you should leverage 30 mini lots at most, even when you can possibly trade more.

CHAPTER 10:

How to Set-up Your Forex Trading Account and Begin Trading

A t this point, you may feel that you can now begin to trade in the foreign exchange market. We have also included other important considerations that you must understand before you open up your forex trading account.

Gearing Up With a Forex Practice Account

For beginners in the forex market, the best way to gear up in this new opportunity is to use a practice account.

Many online forex brokers provide free trials so you can sign up with a trading account and immediately experience real-time price action without spending your own real money first.

In most practice accounts, you will be provided with a virtual cash that you can make trades. The risk will be zero and you can take advantage of the experience as you learn how forex trading works.

With a practice account, you will actually see how prices fluctuate at different times of the day and you can see how currency pairs may vary from each other.

While trading in a practice account, you should alongside monitor the news relevant to the currencies you are trading. This will provide you an insight on how the forex market will react to news releases.

Aside from evaluating the market movement, you may also start trading in real-time conditions in the market without the risk of losing your money and you can also try various trading strategies to see if they work in your condition.

You can also improve your own understanding on how margin trading and leverage works and you can experience managing opening positions and you'll get a chance using various orders.

Most forex brokers will allow 30-day trials when you can also access charts and other technical supplements.

Before you sign up for a full membership, try to open practice accounts first with different forex brokers. Explore different features and capacities of these platforms. Also take note that different forex brokers have different trading policies.

Setting Up a Forex Trading Account

Forex trading is quite similar to stock market trading because you have first to open your own trading account. Similar to the stock market, every forex account as well as the services you can take advantage of can be different. Hence, it is crucial that you look for the most suitable platform for you.

Trading Leverage

When we speak of leverage, we refer to the opportunity to take control of bigger amounts of cash with minimal capital from your own pocket. The leverage level is directly proportional to the risk level. Take note that the leverage amount on a platform could be different according to the features of the account on its own. However, the most popular one is the 50:1 leverage. Some accounts could offer a maximum leverage of 250:1.

For example, a maximum leverage of 100:1 signifies that in each dollar that you hold in the brokerage account, you can use up to $100. For instance, if you have an account balance of $100, the brokerage can allow you to trade as much as $10,000 in the fx. This leverage could also define the total amount that you can hold in your account or your margin for trading a specific amount. In the stock market, the margin is often at 50 per cent and the leverage could be 50:1, which can be at least 2 per cent.

In general, leverage is regarded as a primary advantage of trading in the foreign exchange market, because this will allow you to create substantial gains with minimal capital. But leverage could also have extreme downsides when a trade is moving in the opposite direction, because the losses could also be big.

With this leverage type, there is always the actual probability that your losses are higher than what you have invested, even though most accounts have safeguard stops to prevent the account from hitting negative. As such, it is crucial that you take note of this when you open a brokerage account, and once you identify your preferred leverage, you could understand the involved risks.

Fees and Commissions

Another major advantage of forex platforms is that investing through them could be done through a commission, which is unlike stock market accounts where you need to pay a broker a certain fee for every trade. You are now directly dealing with market players and you don't have to pass through another layer such as brokers.

Every time that you enter a trade, it is the market makers, which can seize the spread. Hence, when the ask/bid for a forex market is 1.5300/50, the market maker can capture between the difference between the points.

In setting up your own forex account, be sure to take note that every firm has various spreads on currency pairs that you trade. Even though they are usually different by only several pips, this could be substantial when you are planning to do a lot of trading. Hence, in setting up an account, be certain that you are aware of the pip and spread of specific currency pairs that you are interested in trading.

Other Factors

You must take note that there are several differences between every forex platform and the programs or software that they are offering. Every forex trading company may offer various levels of programs and services including the fees beyond and above the actual costs of trading. Moreover, because of the less strict conditions in the foreign exchange market, you should find a reliable firm. When you are also not completely confident to trade with real cash, you can also try trading in practice accounts or demos.

How to Start Trading in the Forex Market

After understanding the most crucial factors in opening your own forex account, it is time to look into what specifically you could trade within the platform. The two primary methods in trading in the forex market includes the actual trading (selling and buying) of forex pairs, in which you short a currency and long another.

Another method is via buying the derivatives that monitor the fluctuations of particular currency pair. These strategies are quite similar to the common techniques used in the stock market. Basically, buying and selling the currency pair is the most popular method, much in a similar manner that many traders are buying and selling currency units.

In this setting, a trader may hope that the currency pair's value will change in a profitable way. If you choose to short a pair, it signifies that you are betting on the possibility that the pair's value will fall. For instance, let's assume that you want a short position for the USD/JPY pair.

You can make profits when the value of the fx pair goes down, and you will lose your investment if it rises. This pair will rise if USD increases its price against the JPY, therefore it is actually a trust on the JPY.

Another alternative is to use futures and options, which are derivative products, so you can make money from the currency value changes. If you purchase a currency pair option, you can gain the privilege to buy a pair on a specific rate prior to a setting of point.

Meanwhile, a futures forex contract could build the agreement to purchase the currency pair at a specific point. These trading strategies are often employed by more experienced traders, but as a beginner, you should be aware of them.

Order Types

In looking for a new trading position, you may have to use a market order or a limit order, which are actually similar when you are placing a new position in the stock market. A market order can provide you the capacity to acquire the currency at specific exchange rate that it is presently trading in the foreign exchange market. On the other hand, the limit order will allow you to identify a specific entry price.

If you are already holding an open position in the market, you may have to consider employing a take profit order, so you could lock in your gains. For instance, let us assume that you are already sure that the USD/GBP will react at 1.8700, but you are not completely certain that the price will rise any higher. You can use a take-profit order that will immediately close your position if the price hits 1.8700, which will lock in your profits.

The stop loss order is also a tool that you can use when you want to hold the open positions. This will allow you to figure out if the price could decline prior to the closing of the position and more losses could be accumulated. Hence, if the USD/GBP rate starts to drop, the investor may put a stop-loss, which could halt the position to avoid any further loss. When you are also trading in the stock market, you will realize that the order types that you could enter in the forex trading accounts are quite similar. It is crucial to be familiar with these orders before you actually place your very first trade in the foreign exchange market.

CHAPTER 11:

Tools for Forex Trading

Now we will get into talking about the different platforms and techniques you can use in regards to starting your Forex Trading business. Keep in mind that there are many ways to begin trading using different platforms. We will recommend you some. However, it is your choice which platform you're going to be using for your Forex Trading. Overall, all of them work, and they will yield you the results that you're looking for when it comes to Forex Trading.

Nonetheless, there are over nine platforms what you can use for your Forex Trading needs. With that being said, we're going to go through all those nine trading platforms that will give you a better idea on which one to pick and our opinion on them. The first one we're going to talk about is going to be IG.

IG

This platform has known by many people to be one of the most trusted and well-planned out trading platforms to use for Forex Traders. Many of the top Forex Traders, use this platform for their Forex needs. They have a big list of tradable products and also provide you with excellent rating tools. They are known to be the top in the industry, with both trading tools and education. This is perhaps known to be the best trading platform for Forex traders to use, lowest price, and the most reliable.

Saxo Bank

This bank is also one of the top Forex Trading platforms in the market, not only does have competitive prices, but it comes with excellent trading platforms. It has excellent quality research and has reliable customer service. Meaning of the word traitor swears by this platform, Saxo bank offers the complete package which is worth being a customer for. Many Forex Traders will say that these are the most trustworthy platforms to work with when it comes to Forex Trading.

CMC Markets

Even though this platform has been office regulated, CMC Markets offers Traders one of the most comprehensive ranges of offerings with excellent pricing. It also has the next Generation trading platform, which is very Innovative and attracts a lot of younger Forex Traders into the platform. If you're looking for something that is futuristic and you can have fun with, then most definitely go for a CMC Markets. It has been known to be trustworthy amongst many Forex Traders, so this would be the right choice for you when it comes to starting your Forex Trading.

TD Ameritrade

This is perhaps one of the favorite platforms to trade in. Unfortunately, this is only available in the United States. However, what's nearly 80 currency pairs to trade alongside, and comes with a tremendous amount of trading tools this is no slouch. Moreover, the tools that provide you with the help you to succeed in Forex Trading. One of the safest platforms to work in and comes with excellent customer service. Highly recommended by many top Forex traders who are living in the United States, if you are living in the United States than we would highly recommend that you use this platform for your Forex needs.

Forex.com

This website has plenty of options for Forex Trading and many other Traders. Known to be beginner-friendly many people offer this platform when they're first starting, although we don't recommend that much if you're a beginner then you can most definitely start with this. But remember once you get a little bit better at four trading, you will eventually have to learn more about it and therefore this one be so useful anymore. Nonetheless, this is a great platform to start with when you're starting your forex trading.

CityIndex

This platform is a multi-asset Forex broker, mostly regulated in the UK and Singapore. This offers competitive spreads across multiple trading platforms. The good thing is this broker caters to the client's needs. So, if you do decide to work with them, he will feel more welcomed, and you will be able to manage it a little bit better as compared to another Forex Trading platform. This would be great for beginners as well, as it will help you with the tools you need to succeed in Forex Trading. They also offer many programs for Forex Traders, including a high-volume investor.

XTB

This platform has been trusted by many, and several major Financial Centers have regulated it. Known to be one of the most excellent platform's trades in, it has competitive fitting experience and has fantastic customer service. If you're someone looking to be on top of your game, this platform would be an excellent idea for you. It offers fantastic tools that will help you to succeed in your forex trading needs.

Dukascopy

If you're looking for tools, under this platform offers many of them. More than any of the Forex Trading platforms that will be mentioned, not only that it has incredible market research and therefore can help you to succeed even more in Forex Trading. This would be our second option when it comes to starting your Forex Trading and to pick out a platform, and it is a mobile app that helps you to Forex trade. But also comes the desktop platform, the only problem with this platform is that they don't have too much to offer. Nonetheless, it is a great platform to get started with.

FXCM

If you're looking for a wide range of trading options, then this would be the best platform to go with. But this platform caters to more high-volume Traders, algorithmic raiders overall traders that appreciate tools and quality market research. If you're a beginner, then we would recommend that you stay away from this trading platform, however, once you've gotten your feet wet in Forex Trading then make sure to try the part for me as you will see great results from it.

As you can see, there are many tools which you can use to follow Forex Trading, and overall, these platforms will work for you regardless of which one you pick. Keep in mind that we can recommend specific platforms as we did; however, whichever one fits your need will be the best platform for you. There is no wrong or good platform, and it is merely a preference. However, don't test a lot of platforms too much as It can cause you to lose money. Keep in mind that moving money. A lot can add up with the fees, which is something you don't want to do in the long run. The best thing you can do, like to figure out your needs and find out which platform works best for you. We would still recommend that you start with either IG or TD if you live in the USA. Also, make sure that you find out all the policies that come with these platforms. However, you must understand what platform offers you with more specifically what kind of policies they have. Some systems might not work for you and certain type forms, so make sure, but you understand a strategy before you get into any of these platforms. In regards to technique, the platform you disable dictated what kind of methods you can and cannot use. The great news is that when you're using specific platforms, they will help you to understand and utilize the techniques which will help you to make more money with your Forex Trading. Overall, understand that picking out the right platform for your Forex Trading needs is very important, so make sure you take your time with it and understand what platform you're getting yourself into.

CHAPTER 12:

Sector Analysis and Strategy

There are several types of forex strategies; however, it is important to choose the right one based preferred trading style to trade successfully. Some strategies work on short-term trades as well as long-term trades. The type of Forex strategies you choose depends on a few factors like:

- Entry points - traders need to determine the appropriate time to enter the market

- Exit point-trader need to develop rules on when to exit the market as well as how to get out a losing position

- Time availability

- If you have a full-time job, then you cannot use day trading or scalping styles

- Personal choices

People who prefer lower winning rates but larger gains should go for position trading while those who prefer higher winning rate but smaller gains can choose the swing trading

Common Forex Trading strategies include:

Range trading strategy

Range trading is one of the many viable trading strategies. This strategy is where a trader identifies the support and resistance levels and buys at the support level and sells at the resistance level. This strategy works when there is a lack of market direction or the absence of a trend. Range trading strategies can be broken down into three steps:

Finding the Range

Finding the range uses the support and resistance zones. The support zone is the buying price of the security while the resistance zone price is the selling price of a security. A breakout happens in the event that the price goes beyond the trading range, whereas a breakdown occurs in the event that the price goes below the trading range.

Time Your Entry

Traders use a variety of indicators like price action and volume to enter and exit the trading range. They can also use oscillators like CCI, RSI, and stochastics to time their entry. The oscillators track prices using mathematical calculations. Then the traders wait for the prices to reach the support or resistance zones. They often strike when the momentum turns price in the opposing direction.

Managing Risk

The last step is risk management. When the level of support or resistance breaks, traders will want to exit any range-based positions. They can either use a stop loss above the previous high or invert the process with a stop below the current low.

Pros

- There are ranges that can last even for years producing multiple winning trades.

Cons

- Long-lasting ranges are not easy to come by, and when they do, every range trader wants to use it.

- Not all ranges are worth trading

Trend Trading Strategy

Another popular and common Forex Trading strategy is the trend trading strategy. This strategy attempts to make profits by analyzing trends. The process involves identifying an upward or downward trend in a currency price movement and choosing trade entry and exit points based on the currency price within the trend.

Trend traders use these four common indicators to evaluate trends; moving averages, relative strength index (RSI), On-Balance-Volume (OBV), and Moving Average Convergence Divergence (MACD). These indicators provide trend trade signals, warn of reversals, and simplify price information. A trader can combine several indicators to trade.

Pros

- Offers a better risk to reward
- Can be used across any markets

Cons
- Learning to trade on indicators can be challenging.

Pairs Trade

This is a neutral trading strategy, which allows pair traders to gain profits in any market conditions. This strategy uses two key strategies:

- Convergence trading - this strategy focuses on two historically correlated securities, where the trader buys one asset forward and sells a similar asset forward for a higher price anticipating that prices will become equal. Profits are made when the underperforming position gains value, and the outperforming position's price deflates
- Statistical trading - this is a short-term strategy that uses the mean reversion models involving broadly diversified Security

Portfolios. This strategy uses data mining and statistical methods.

Pros
- If pair trades go as expected investors can make profits

Cons
- This strategy relies on a high statistical correlation between two securities, which can be a challenge.
- Pairs trade relies a lot on historical trends, which do not depict future trends accurately.

Price Action Trading

This Forex Trading strategy involves analyzing the historical prices of securities to come up with a trading strategy. Price action trading can be used in short, medium, and long periods. The most commonly used price action indicator is the price bar, which shows detailed information like high and low-price levels during a specific period. However, most traders use more than one strategy to recognize trading patterns, stop-losses, and entry, and exit levels. Technical analysis tools also help price action traders make decisions.

Pros
- No two traders will interpret certain price action the same way

Cons
- Past price history cannot predict future prices accurately

Carry Trade Strategy

Carry trade strategy involves borrowing a low-interest currency to buy a currency that has a high rate; the goal is to make a profit with the interest rate difference. For example, one can buy currency pairs like the Japanese yen (low interest) and the Australian dollar (high interest) because the interest rate spreads are very high. Initially, carry trade was used as a one-way trade that moved upwards without reversals, but carry traders soon discovered that everything went downhill once the trade collapsed.

With the carry trade strategy:

- You need to first identify which currencies offer high rates and which ones have low rates.
- Then match two currencies with a high-interest differential
- Check whether the pair has been in an upward tendency favoring the higher-interest rate currency

Pros

- The strategy works in a low volatility environment.
- Suitable for a long-term strategy

Cons

- Currency rates can change anytime
- Ricky because they are highly leveraged
- Used by many traders therefore overcrowded

Momentum Trading

This strategy involves buying and selling assets according to the strength of recent price trends. The basis for this strategy is that an asset price that is moving strongly in a given direction will continue to move in the same direction until the trend loses strength. When assets reach a higher price, they tend to attract many investors and traders who push the market price even higher. This continues until large pools of sellers enter the market and force the asset price down. Momentum traders identify how strong trends are in a given direction. They open positions to take advantage of the expected price change and close positions when the prices go down.

There are two kinds of momentum:

1. Relative momentum - different securities within the same class are compared against each other, and then traders and investors buy strong performing ones and sell the weak ones.

2. Absolute momentum - an asset's price is compared against its previous performance.

Pros

- Traders can capitalize on volatile market trends
- Traders can gain high profit over a short period
- This strategy can take advantage of changes in stock prices caused by emotional investors.

Cons

- A momentum investor is always at a risk of timing a buy incorrectly.
- This strategy works best in a bull market; therefore, it is market sensitive
- This strategy is time-intensive; investors need to keep monitoring the market daily.
- Prices can shift in a different direction anytime

Pivot Points

This strategy determines resistance and support levels using the average of the previous trading sessions, which predict the next prices. They take the average of the high, low, and closing prices. A pivot point is a price level used to indicate market movements. Bullish sentiment occurs when one trades above the pivot point while bearish sentiment occurs when one trades below the pivot point.

Pros

- Traders can use the levels to plan out their trading in advance because prices remain the same throughout the day

- Works well with other strategies

Cons

- Some traders do not find pivot points useful

- There is no guarantee that price will stop or reverse at the levels created on the chart

CHAPTER 13:

What a Beginner Needs to Know About Forex Trading

Forex trading is an avenue that is making people earn a more significant income. There are many platforms where you can put that little penny in the trading and amerce that profits. However, it needs you to be that wise speculator who knows who reads the indicator promptly and knows the point to make that trading.

Remember that Forex trading is all about the trading of currencies. Therefore, you have to be knowledgeable about how the different currencies perform. The following are the basics where a beginner should know.

You should first be interested in knowing how the currencies behave in the market. That is where one ought to recognize the values of different currencies. The major currencies traded across the globe shows significant value in the market. Some of these currencies include the Us Dollar, Sterling Pound, Swiss Franc, Japanese Yen and the Euro.

That is not to say that other currencies are not traded but this one has the commanding value in the Forex trade. Therefore, it requires the broker and the trader to be updated on the value of the stated monies. This is because at some instances the currencies may deteriorate and increase their worth significantly. Another thing to contemplate is how the paired currencies behave with each other. For example, in the Forex chart you may see the Us Dollar combined with the Euro or any other pair.

Another thing you ought to know is the type of indicators available and how one can make trading. These indicators follow specific movement criteria. First and foremost, before knowing that indicator thinks of the scales used in the chart. The chart represents a graphical diagram with both the independent and the depend scales.

The independent scales are normally plotted on the horizontal axis and the dependent scale on the vertical axis. Therefore, you have to know the different variables in the trading. Some of these variables are the price movement, the volume, and many others. Check on this chart's ad test the movement of these variables appropriately.

Concerning the indicators, you should be aware of how these indicators behave. They are of different types and are influenced by the variables you use. For a beginner it is essential to have that knowledge of how they behave is crucial. You have to know the different types of these indicators so that you can follow their trend.

Think of the indicators like the Moving Average Convergence and Divergence. This indicator measures the two exponential moving averages. There is the Bollinger band indicator that measures the standard deviation those currencies of the currencies. Some terms like the volatility market you also need to know them. Remember that the volatility of the currency is its behavior to have either a sharp increase or decrease in the market. That is where you can either gain a sizable profit or loss.

That is not to forget the relative strength index which is beneficial for ascertaining the overbought and the oversold. These indicators are very many in particular, but when you have their information is nothing that should stop you from earning.

Even the types of charts like the candlesticks, line charts and bar charts should be at your fingertips. There are different charts for every level of your trading. For example, in your case as the beginner, you can use the candlestick or the basic charts.

Another thing is the trend analysis. You should analyze the direction which the indicator flows whenever you make a trade. That should help you in analyzing the peak times and recession periods of a paired currency. You also can anticipate the next performance of the paired currency if you are experienced in reading the behaviors of the indicators.

You still use this information to know the right point of the market entry and the exits of the point. Those brokers who analyze the trend accordingly and are in a position of obtaining a sizeable return.

Which Qualities Make You as The Beginner Successful in The Trading

After knowing the basic you do not just start trading when you have the minimal qualities required in this business. You will realize how you will get frustrated when you stake a lot of cash then the trading fails. At other junctures you need to apply essential speculation tactics. That is the knowledge of probability and analyzing the statistics for you to stand a chance in trading. Some of these qualities are.

Be that guy who is good in decision making. Remember that the facility needs intelligence and critical thinking. You may find yourself succeeding a lot in particular segment of trading. However not to realize that it may be a trap where even after making sublime returns you will eventually gain a hefty loss.

Some other times you need not consider only short-term profit but fight for long-term returns. You may identify a promising venture but where whose returns are realized in long-term basis. However, if you are that person who needs quick money you will not be patient on that venture, but look for short-term profits. Moreover, those who take time in making a decision realizes a pattern trend and makes the right move.

Be that risk-taker who do not fear to make a loss. If all people were risk-averse, then there would no Forex trading. Hey, remember that this business is like a gamble. Am sure many people do not like hearing this term, but whenever you are dealing with uncertainties you are gambling. No matter what you do you have to sacrifice that penny expecting two possibilities which are either a win or a loss? Even other renowned investors cite that 'you have to stake big to win big'. Therefore, be a risk-taker who stakes big and hopes for massive earnings of returns. Even if you fail seldom, do not give up, as eventually you will win.

Persistent is another quality required for you beginners in the Forex trading. When you are persistent you normally are tolerant. You never give up hope even after failing many times. Why your needs are learning from mistakes. Do not repeat the same strategy that you did which failed you. Be that person who sees the failure as a lesson to improve their ways of staking.

Adopt a trial and error strategy which will eventually give you a winning edge. You do not expect keep winning all the time, you will undoubtedly lose in some instances. You will realize you will keep developing tactics of trading with this trial and error strategy. You will too familiarize yourself with the trend analysis. Therefore, what is stopping you from knowing how to make that currencies trade.

Timing is also operational in the business. You have to flexible enough to identify a profitable opportunity. The way the currencies behave is like a pendulum that goes in every direction. You can use a stopwatch and identify the specific time the trading signals a return and risks or an entry point or an exit point. Those seconds or minutes you waste may be the advent of your failure. Do a demo trade which you do not have to input some cash? Look at the behavior of the currency and how they react in any substantial change. You may identify the correct timing when you need to stake. Therefore, you will have that confidence to stake your money in the trading.

What are the steps for a beginner in trading?

First, you have to have good preparations. Trading does not fall on the moon, however you need to have the proper tools for trading. You need to have an electronic device, it can be your phone, laptop, iPad or any other gadget that can connect to the Internet. Make sure you have the best source for Internet connection because you need to make many references to the currencies from the network. Make sure you are comfortably seated and good to go.

Choose the best agency company in Forex trading. Remember there are many companies online that broker those currencies. Before choosing a firms one should conduct an extensive study of them. You also need to consider if they are registered and licensed. Moreover, consider their brokerage fee and their essential features. It should have the necessary charts, variables and indicators that satisfy the trader. Consult other traders to recommend the best brokerage firm. When you are satisfied with this you can create an account with them. Find out if they provide a demo account which is necessary for trading practice.

The demo account is very vital for you to practice trading. Remember, you cannot put your money into a venture that you do not know, therefore you must understand it first. If you are satisfied with it then start the trading program. The good thing with a demo account is that you are not afraid of any risks since you have not staked any cash. Check with the trading platform and its charts.

Open the chart or the diagram and try to choose a currency pair. Most of the times the currencies are found in the top of the graph, on its sides or the below the graph. Look at the available currencies and think about them. You have to be keen in choosing the pair. You can even do research on the values of different currencies and how they behave with each other. Do not forget to check their volatility and how they fair when traded. Choose those pairs and fix them at the graph.

Then choose the indicators you like. Indicators are of different types and it is upon you the trader to examine which you will understand. You can use the Moving Average Convergence and Divergence which measure the exponential averages. You may think of the Bollinger band in the standard deviation or the RSI which identifies the overbought or the oversold. If you don't understand them ask an expert to teach you.

Place the order if you feel you are ready for that trade. Prioritize price as the main element in harnessing a profit from the currencies. With the currencies, pairs evaluate how the indicators move. They may move in different directions or together. You have to know the peak time and the recession times.

When the waves are on a higher point that is the peak period and when they are low then that is the lower period. Select your value and see the behavior and you will realize whether it is a return or a loss. If the pair disappoints you, then choose another and repeat the same action. That is until you are convinced of the best pair of trading currencies.

Doing a lot of practice with a demo and will help you realize a trend. Therefore, conduct an effective trend analysis that should help you to predict the exact behavior of the pair currency. You will also know the point to amerce greater profit and big losses. Also, the trend analysis will help you to identify the specific points where you can exit the trade with a profit.

When you are satisfied with the demo you can stake the amount and follow the same procedures. Be accurate and persistent and try many times even if you fail.

CHAPTER 14:

What Do You Do If the Market Is Going In The Wrong Direction?

Pay Attention to Daily Pivot Points

Forex traders should watch daily pivot points closely. This is especially important for day traders. However, it is also important for swing traders, position traders, and even traders who focus on long-term positions. It is important to do so because tons of other forex traders do the same.

In a certain way, pivot trading is like a self-fulfilling prophecy. Essentially, markets often find resistance or support at pivot points since thousands of pivot traders place orders at those points. Consequently, when a large volume of trading moves happens at these points or levels, there is no other reason for the move except that many traders placed orders expecting such a move.

However, pivot points should not be the only basis of a Forex Trading strategy. Rather, regardless of one's strategy, one should watch these points for signs of either potential market or continuation of a trend. Forex traders should look at pivot levels and the trading activities that take place around them as a confirming indicator to use in conjunction with their chosen strategy.

Define Trading Style and Goals

Before setting out on any journey, travelers need to have a clear idea of where they are going and how to get to their destination. In the same way, forex traders need to have clear goals, in addition to ensuring that their trading strategies will help them achieve those goals.

Each Forex Trading style or strategy comes with a different risk profile. Therefore, traders who want to win in Forex Trading need to find and adopt the right approach and attitude to trade profitably. Those who cannot imagine going to sleep with an open market position, for example, should consider focusing on day trading.

Forex traders with funds they believe will benefit from a trade appreciation over several months; on the other hand, they should think about position trading. Essentially, it is important for a forex trader to determine whether his/her personality will fit any particular trading strategy. Any mismatch will probably lead to certain losses and stress.

Trade with an Edge

Successful forex traders only risk their hard-earned money when a market opportunity provides them with an edge. In other words, they do so when the opportunity presents them with something that will boost the chances of their trades being successful. This edge can be various things, even a simple thing, such as selling at a price level that one identifies as strong resistance.

Forex traders can also increase their probability of success and their edge by having several technical factors in their favor. If the 100-period, 50-period, and 10-period moving averages all meet at the same price level, for example, it will likely offer significant resistance or support for a market because many traders will be acting together by trading off any of those averages.

Converging technical indicators also provide a similar edge. This happens when different indicators on many periods converge to provide resistance or support. Having the price hit an identified resistance or support level, in addition to having price movement at that level, is an indication of a potential market reversal.

The Trading Platform and Broker

Forex traders should spend adequate time researching a suitable trading platform and a reputable broker. It is important to identify and understand the difference between brokers and determine how each of them goes about making a market, as well as their policies. Trading the exchange-driven market, for example, is different from trading in the spot market or OTC market.

Traders should also choose the trading platform that fits the analysis they want to do. Traders who want to use Fibonacci numbers to trade, for example, should ensure the trading platform they choose has the ability to draw Fibonacci lives. A good platform with a bad broker is just as bad as a poor trading platform with a good broker. Therefore, forex traders need to find the best of both.

Preserve Capital

It is more important for traders to avoid huge losses than to make huge profits. For people who are new to Forex Trading, this concept may not sound quite right. However, it is important to understand that winning in Forex Trading means knowing how to preserve or protect one's capital.

According to the founder of Tudor Corporation, Paul Tudor Jones, playing great defense is the most important rule of trading. Actually, he is a great trader to learn from and study. In addition to building a hugely successful hedge fund, Tudor Jones has an excellent record of profitable trading.

He also played an important role in creating the ethics-training program needed to gain membership in all futures exchanges in the United States. Protecting the trading capital, or playing great defense, is very important in Forex Trading because many people who venture into Forex Trading are unable to continue trading as a result of running out of money.

Many forex traders drain their accounts soon after they make a few trades. Having strict risk management practices is important for people who want to win in Forex Trading. Traders who manage to preserve their trading capital are able to continue trading for as long as they want to, and might eventually become huge winners.

One great trade can fall into a trader's lap and significantly increase his/her profits and account size. One does not need to be the smartest trader in the world to make money in the forex market. If nothing else, the luck of the draw can have traders who manage to protect their capital stumble into trades that generate enough profits to make their trading careers a huge success.

Small Losses and Focus

After forex traders fund their trading accounts, they need to understand that their capital is at risk. Therefore, they should not depend on that money for their daily living expenses. Actually, it is better to think of those funds as vacation funds. Once their vacation is over, their money is gone.

Having this trading attitude will help prepare them to accept and learn from small losses, which will also help them manage their risk better. Forex traders should focus on their trades and accept small losses, which are normal in any type of business, rather than constantly and obsessively focusing on their equity.

Simple Technical Analysis

Consider this example of two forex traders in extremely different situations. The first trader has a specially designed trading computer with several monitors, a large office, swanky furnishings, trading charts, and market news feeds. He also has several moving averages, technical indicators, momentum indicators, and much more.

The other trader, on the other hand, works from a relatively simple office space and uses a regular desktop or laptop computer. His charts reveal just one or two technical indicators on the price action of the market.

Most people would consider the first trader to be more professional and extremely successful, and they would probably be wrong in their assumption. Actually, the second trader is closer to the image of a forex trader who wins consistently. Traders can apply numerous forms of technical analysis to a chart. Having more, however, does not necessarily mean having better.

Using a huge number of indicators might actually make things more complicated and confusing for a forex trader. They amplify indecision and doubt, causing him/her to miss many potentially profitable trades. Therefore, it is better to have a simple trading strategy with just a few rules, as well as a minimum of indicators to consider.

A few very successful forex traders make money from the forex market almost every day without using any technical indicators overlaid on their charts. They achieve this impressive feat without taking advantage of a relative strength indicator, trend lines, trading robots, moving averages, or expert advisors. Their market analysis involves a simple candlestick chart.

Weekend Analysis

The forex market ceases operation on the weekend. Therefore, forex traders should use this time to study their weekly charts to identify news or patterns that could affect their trades in either a positive or a negative way. This will give the objectivity, which will help them make smarter trading plans.

Placing Stop-Loss Orders at the Right Price Levels

In addition to protecting one's capital in case of a losing trade, this strategy is also an important aspect of smart Forex Trading. Many newcomers to the forex market assume that risk management simply means placing stop-loss orders close to the entry point of their trades. This is partly accurate; however, habitually placing stop-loss orders too close to their trade entry points is something that might contribute to their lack of success.

Sometimes, stop-loss orders can stop a trade, only to see the market make a reversal in favor of the trade. It is common for novice traders to endure watching this happen. Sometimes, this reversal proceeds to a level that would have seen them gain a sizable profit if the stop-loss order had not terminated the trade.

Obviously, traders should enter trades that allow them to place stop-loss orders close enough to their trade entry points to avoid making huge losses. However, they should place them at a reasonable price level, based on their analysis of the market. When it comes to reasonable placement of stop-loss orders, the general rule of thumb is to place them a bit further than the price the market should not trade at, based on market analysis.

Use a Consistent Methodology

Before a prospective trader enters the forex market, he/she needs to have a good idea of how he/she will make trading decisions. Essentially, forex traders should know the information they will need to make smart decisions on entering a trade or exiting one. Some traders choose to analyze a chart and the fundamental of the economy to decide the best time to trade.

Others, however, prefer to perform technical analysis to determine the ideal time to execute a trade. Whichever methodology or strategy a trader chooses to employ, he/she needs to be consistent and ensure the chosen methodology is adequately adaptive. In other words, it should be flexible enough to handle the forex market's changing dynamics.

Choosing the Right Entry and Exit Points

Most inexperienced forex traders do not know how to judge conflicting information that often presents when analyzing charts in various timeframes. Certain information, for example, might indicate a sell signal on a weekly chart, but show up as a purchasing opportunity in an intraday chart.

Therefore, if a trader is using a weekly chart to determine his/her basic trading direction and a daily chart to tie his/her entry, then he/she should try to synchronize the two charts. If the weekly chart is providing a buy signal, for example, he/she should wait for the daily chart to confirm this signal. In other words, keeping signal timing in sync is a good tip for winning in Forex Trading.

CHAPTER 15:

The Right Approach

In order to be successful in currency trading, you definitely need to make sure that you are approaching things the right way. First is understanding that you are in this for the long haul. That means that you understand that you are not going to turn your $10,000 to $100,000 in two or three weeks by engaging in three or four trades every day. Sure, you could try that, but if that strategy worked then the internet would be littered with tales of how this unemployed dad or that soccer mom made $100,000 in two weeks trading currency and there haven't been any stories like that—at least none that we have heard of. Currency trading is a long-term investment. You make a trade today based on an informed decision on a particular currency and perhaps you hold onto that currency for three weeks, patiently waiting as it slowly rises in value: three pips, four pips, 12 pips. Meanwhile, as you did not invest all of your capital on that trade, perhaps later in the week you engage in a second trade with a plan of holding onto that currency for a little while, too. Perhaps as soon as you purchase this second currency you see that it begins to fall. As you have established a threshold at which you will sell your currency (as part of a trading plan), you end up selling that currency for a slight loss. That's three trades in a week's time. Not three trades in a single day, but in a week.

Being successful at currency trading requires this sort of approach. You have to be patient. Just as a president or other government official has to be patient in order to see the changes that he or she has instituted take effect over time, so too will you have to be patient as the currency you traded for rises in value, falls, and then rises again We mentioned briefly the importance of having a trading plan. Many professional traders have a trading plan (if not most of them), in part because they have a superior that they are answering to and that superior wants to know that they are actually using that money wisely. Having a trading plan has been shown to work for professional traders and it will certainly work for you, an independent retail trader. Think about it this way: you are not investing your company's money; you are investing your own. Shouldn't you be doing at least what the professional traders are doing, if not more? If they are investing in a real-time news source and coming up with a trading plan then you should be doing at least that much.

A trading plan does not have to be something extremely elaborate. You will have to decide what's important for you to know down the line when you are trying to figure out why you bought so much Thai baht when the news reports from the day prior suggested that actually, you should have bought South Korean won. Your plan should explain why you are buying this currency vs that based on concrete information that you have (like the resolution of a political crisis, foreign investment, revised economic forecasts, etc.). Your plan should also go into how long you plan to hold onto that currency and why. Perhaps your plan will also explain the conditions under which you might sell. For example, perhaps you planned to hold on to those Japanese yen for two weeks, but the value has increased so rapidly that you feel you need to sell after only one week as it is likely that the value will have fallen if you wait to reach the two-week mark. Your trading plan could easily take the format of explaining where the yen is today, when you plan to purchase yen, when you plan to sell, and at what threshold you will sell early if the yen rises or falls quicker than you imagined.

The purpose of a trading plan isn't to waste your time or to bore you with the intricacies of an endeavor that you expected to be quick, easy, and fun. Currency trading, like the stock market, is subject to vicissitudes. It is not enough to have capital, a broker, and a news source. You may have all that and still lose money. You need to have a trading plan. Again, this is for no one's benefit, but your own. This plan will not only guide you on making informed, well-thought-out decisions on the foreign exchange market, it may also prevent you from making stupid ones, like engaging in more trades than you need to. Once you have a solid plan, and once you understand the idea that you are in this game for the long haul, then you have embarked on the first step towards success in currency trading.

The Importance of a Trading Plan

It is important first to settle your trading style before you start developing your forex trading plan. Various trading styles basically call for variations on trading plans, even though there are a lot of overarching rules in trading that are applicable to all styles.

Time Frame
You need to determine how long you would hold your position. Some forex traders look at short-term trade opportunities. This is known as day trading. Meanwhile, some traders are trying to capture more significant movements in forex prices over days, weeks or even months.

Currency Pair
Are you looking to trade in different currency pairs or are you more interested to focus your energy into few pairs?

Risk Appetite
How much money are you willing to risk and what is your level of expectations for your trading profits?

Rationale
Are you technically or fundamentally inclined? Are you looking to develop a systematic trading model? What strategies are you looking to follow? Are you comfortable in following forex trends? Or are you more inclined to become a breakout forex trader?

Don't worry if you still don't have answers to these questions. Hopefully as you read this book, you can choose the forex trading approach you are interested to pursue.

You can try different strategies and styles by using demo accounts. But don't forget that your goal is to zero in your trading style that you feel comfortable with and that you can pursue regularly.

In addition, you also need to consider other factors such as your individual circumstances such as personal discipline, temperament, finances, free time, family, and work obligations. These are essential variables and you are the only one who knows how they impact your forex trading.

Regardless of the trading style you choose to pursue, achieving success can be challenging if you don't set your trade plan then follow it. Remember, trade plans will help you avoid losing a lot of money from bad trades and can also help you win big in the market.

Moreover, your trading plan serves as your guide, which helps you explore the trades after the emotions and adrenaline begin pumping regardless of what the market presents to you. But this doesn't mean that forex trading is any easier compared to other financial markets.

However, it is proven that trading with a plan will significantly improve the probability of your success in the forex market over time. Also, you need to understand that trading without a plan is a guaranteed way to lose money in the forex market.

Sure, you may make money from a few trades, but a day of reckoning will eventually come to any trader who is only guided by his guts. This is always the trend in any financial markets.

The starting line of any trading plan is to determine an opportunity for trading. Do not wait for any writing on the wall that will tell you what and when to trade. You must devote your effort and energy in looking for lucrative opportunities for trading.

CHAPTER 16:

Choosing a Broker

A broker refers to a firm or an individual who charges a certain fee or rather a commission for executing the buying and the selling process. In other words, they play the role of connecting the customer and the seller of the product. Thus, they are generally paid for acting as a link between the two parties.

For instance, a client might be willing to buy shares from a particular organization. However, he might be lacking enough information about the places that he can purchase these shares. Thus, he will be forced to seek a person who understands the stock trade markets well. The broker will, therefore, educate the client as well as link them with the right sellers. The broker will thus earn by offering such a connection.

List of Common Brokers

IG

It is rated as one of the best Forex brokers in the world. It was one of the pioneers in offering contracts for difference as well as spread beating. The organization was founded in the year 1974 and had been growing as a leader in online trading as well as the marketing industry.

One of the features that have boosted its growth is the fact that it has linked a lot of customers, hence gaining more trust. In other words, a duet to its large customer base, a lot of clients prefers selling and buying their services.

The other feature worth noting is that this organization is London based, and it is among one of the companies that are listed on the London Stock Trade market for more than 250 times. The feature is due to the fact that it offers more than 15,000 products across several asset classes.

Such classes include CFDs on shares, Forex, commodities, bonds, crypto currencies as well as indices. Another feature worth noting is that the 2019 May report, the firm is serving more than 120,000 active clients around the globe. Also, there are more than 350,000 clients that are served on a daily basis. The feature has been critical in boosting its expansion as this group of individuals does more advertisements.

Some of the benefits that one gains by working in this industry are the fact that it allows comprehensive trading and the utilization of tools that enhance the real trade of data. The other feature worth noting is that it has a public traded license that allows a regular jurisdiction across the entire globe. In other words, one can acquire the services of this organization across the whole world with ease without the fear of acting against the laws of the nation.

Also, the premises offer some of the competitive based commission that enhances pricing as spreading of Forex. There is also a broad range of markets that are associated with the premises too, there several currencies and multi assets CFDs that are offered by the organization. The feature has been critical in the sense that it allows the perfect utilization of all the services as well as the resources available across the globe. Some of the services that are offered by the organization are permitted globally, such that even after traveling from one nation to the other, one can still access their services. Since the year 1974, the organization has joined more than 195,000 traders across the entire globe. The feature has allowed the selling of its shares as well as services, hence its fame.

Saxo Bank
The Forex broker was established in 1992and has then been among the leading organization in offering Forex services as well as the multi-asset brokerages across more than 15 nations. Some of these nations include the UK, Denmark, and Singapore, among others. One of the

features of the organization is that it offers services to both retailers as well as institutional clients in the globe. The appeal has allowed the premises to provide more than one million transactions each day. Thus, it holds over $ 16 billion in asset management.

The Saxo bank also offers more services to all of her clients. Such services include Spot FX, Non-deliverable Forwards (NDFs), contract difference as well as all the stock trade options. The feature has been critical in increasing its customer base across the globe. Some of the services such as crypto and bond services offered in the premises has allowed its expansion in the sense that they are sensitive and essentials.

Some of the benefits that one gain by assessing the services of the premises are that it enhances diverse selection of quality, it increases competitive commissions and Forex spread as well as an improved multiple financial jurisdiction function that is allowed across the entire globe. In other words, the premises offer services allowed worldwide, and that considers the rules and policies provided in each nation. The feature has enhanced its continued growth despite the increased competition.

One must pay a minimum deposit of about $2,000 and have an automated trading solution for all the traders. There are times when the premises offer bonuses of 182 trade Forex pairs to all its clients. This feature has also been the key reason behind its increased expansion. In other words, there are various services offered at a relatively low price, hence the widening of its customer base.

CMC Markets
The premises were founded in 1989 and since then, it has grown to be one of the leading retail Forex, as well as a CFD brokerage. The premises thus serve more than 10,000 CFD instruments that cut across all the classes such as Forex, commodities as well as security markets. The feature has allowed the premises to spread its services to more than 60,000 clients across the entire globe.

The premises have more than 15 offices that are well distributed in the nation; it offers the services. Most of its actions are thus related in UK, Australia as well as Canada. The feature is due to the fact that the premises have customer bases in some of these nations. In other words, its services are well accepted in Canada and the UK.

There are various benefits one gains by joining the premises. One, the premise offers some of the best competitive spread to all her customers. In other words, there are a variety of services that one can choose from. Also, the premises offer some of the largest selection of currency pairs in the entire industry. There are more than one hundred and eighty currencies that one can access by joining the premises.

The other feature worth noting is that the premises offer some of the best regulated financial agents in the entire globe. In other words, there are policies as well as rules that govern the provision of services in the world. Also, it is easy to identify the premises as there are potent charts as well as patterns that are used as recognition tools.

City Index

This Forex broker was founded in 1983 in the UK. Since then, the premises have gained popularity and has turned out to be one of the leading brokers in London. It is worth noting that in 2015, the premises acquired GAIN Capital Holding Company that enhanced its increased customer base. Since 2015, the premises have been providing traders with services such as CFDs and spreading-betting derivatives. The premises have been further expanding the Forex services with the acquisition of markets as well as FX solutions before gaining the capital market. Nowadays, the City Index has been operating as an independent brand under GAIN Capital in Asia as well as the UK. The feature has allowed a multi-asset solution hence offering traders access to over 12,000 products across the global markets.

Some of the benefits that one gains part of the capital holding, a large selection of CFDs as well as regulated in several jurisdictions. The organization has tight spreads as well as low margins and fast execution. In others, the premises have been time from time, offering average ranges to all the clients; hence its increased customer base.

XTB Review

The organization was founded in Poland in the year 2002. Since then the organization has been well known for its Forex and CFDs brokerage. Since then, the organization has maintained its offices in several nations; it offers its services. The premise has been working as a multi-asset broker that is regulated in several centers, hence increasing their competitive advantage. The premises have been trading as multiple financial centers offering a lot of services to all her traders.

Signs of Illegitimate Brokers

Although numerous brokers have been working in the Forex industry, the feature of legitimacy has been an issue affecting the progress of some these premises. One of the elements that are considered is the vulnerability of the clients. In most cases illegitimate brokers tend to rob their customers. Most of them are self-reliant and optimistic. Most of them operate above their financial knowledge, hence making numerous mistakes. Most of these organization record big loses as they are relatively weak in term of management. The organization offers a lot of transactions that tend to be cumbersome in terms of management. It is worth noting that most of their operations aren't legitimate and never approved by the necessary authorities.

Thus, when deciding on the kind of Forex premises to seek services from, it is essential to consider some factors. Avoid assumptions that are exaggerative in terms of offering services that are above their knowledge. The feature is harmful in the sense that they provide services that are not well planned, hence recording a number of loses that befalls many clients in the long run. In other words, the drops recorded in the organization.

CHAPTER 17:

Benefits of Forex Trading

There are many benefits to trading in forex markets. Let us look at some of them.

Liquidity

The first and most important benefit of forex trading is its liquidity. As you know, the forex market is extremely liquid meaning you can sell your currency at any time. There will be a lot of takers for it, as they will be looking to buy the particular currency. The highly liquid market can help you avoid any loss as you don't have to wait on your currency to be sold. And all of it is automatic. You only have to give the sell order, and within no time your entire order will be sold.

Timing

The forex market is open 24 hours a day, which makes it a great place to invest at. You can keep trading during the day and also during the night if you are dealing with a country's currency whose day timings coincide with your night timings. You can come up with a schedule that will allow you to conveniently trade with all of the different countries that lie in the different time zones. You can also quickly sell off a bad currency without having to wait the whole night or day.

Returns

The rate of returns in foreign currency trade is quite high. You will see that it is possible for you to invest just $10 and control as much as $1000 with it. All you have to do is look for the best currency pairs and start buying and selling them

The leverage that these investments provide is always on the higher side, which makes them an ideal investment avenue for both beginners and old hands.

Costs

The transaction costs of this type of trade are very low. You don't have to worry about big fees when you buy and sell foreign currencies. That is the one big concern that most stock traders have, as they will worry about having to shell out a lot of money towards transaction costs. But that worry is eliminated in currency exchanges, and you can save on quite a lot of money just by choosing to invest in currency.

Non-Directional Trade

The forex market follows a non-directional trade. This means that it does not matter if the difference in the currencies is going upwards or downwards, you will always have the chance to remain with a profit. This is mostly because there is scope for you to short a deal or go long on it depending on the situation and rate of difference. You will understand how this works as and when you partake in it. The main aim of investing in forex is to remain with a steady profit, which is only possible if you know when to hold on to an investment and when to sell it off. This very aspect is seen as being a buffer by traders and is the main reason for them choosing to invest in forex.

Middlemen Eliminated

With forex trade, it is possible for you to eliminate any middlemen. These middlemen will unnecessarily charge you a fee and your costs with keeping piling up. So, you can easily avoid these unnecessary costs and increase your profit margin. These middlemen need not always be brokers and can also be other people who will simply get in the way of your trade just to make a quick buck out of it. You have to be careful and stave such people off in order to avoid any unnecessary costs that they will bring about. Education is key here and the more you know, the better your chances of avoiding any such frauds.

No Unfair Trade

There is no possibility of anyone rich investor controlling the market. This is quite common in the stock market where a single big investor will end up investing a lot of money in a particular stock and then withdraw from it quickly and affect the market negatively. This is not a possibility in the foreign currency market as there is no scope for a single large trader to dominate the market. These traders will all belong to different countries, and it will not be possible for them to control the entire market as a whole. There will be free trade, and you can make the most use of it.

No Entry Barrier

There is no entry barrier, and you can enter and exit the market at any time you like. There is also no limit on the investment amount that you can enter with. You have to try and diversify your currency investments in a way that you minimize your risk potential and increase your profit potential. You can start out with a small sum and then gradually increase it as you go.

Certainty

There is a certain security attached to foreign currencies. You will have the chance to avail guaranteed profits if you invest in currency pairs that are doing well. These can be surmised by going through all the different currency pairs that are doing well in the market. With experience, you will be able to cut down on your losses with ease and also increase your profits. You have to learn from your experience and ensure that you know exactly what you are doing.

Easy Information

Information on the topic of foreign currencies is easily available on the internet and from other sources. This information can be utilized to invest in the best currency pairs. You have to do a quick search of which two pairs are doing well and invest in them without wasting too much time. If you need any other information on the topic, then this book will guide you through it. You can directly go to the topic that you seek and look at the details to provide there.

Apart from these, there are certain other benefits like minimal commission charged by the OTC agent and instant execution of your market orders. No agency will be able to control the foreign exchange market.

These form the different benefits of trading in the forex market but are not limited to just these. You will be acquainted with the others as and when you start investing in it.

CHAPTER 18:

Time Management and Money Management

Time Management

Time management, a key aspect in forex trading, is one of the determinants of the gains and losses a trader is to make from the opening and the close of a trading period. It is therefore paramount that a trader has a solid plan in his or her time management in trading to reap off gains. A trader has to know when to enter and exit the market when to get the necessary information on trading patterns, these and many more being among the aspects of time management of a forex trader.

Match your personality and your trading pattern with the time you have

It is suicidal for a trader to operate on the basis of a trading pattern that does not suit their personality and goes against them in all odds. The personality type being referred to in this case is major whether the trader is patient or not. An impatient trader will want to have instant results and gains for trades made and will therefore not tarry around for trading systems that are long term. Such traders do not find the trade analysis tools that are long term to be useful to their course. Impatient traders are mostly associated with swing traders who get antsy and do not stay put to trade for the long term. Analysis tools that evaluate for long term trade may not be suitable for such traders. Short term analysis tools are mostly preferred for such traders and will work perfectly to their trading plan.

Analysis tools and trading patterns that work for the long term are applicable to those whose personality is being patient. Long term strategies work for these kinds of people. They should, however, take caution not to be blind to current events that may drastically and completely change the trading pattern in existence and therefore results in losses for them. Their strategy also has to be within a time frame that they are comfortable trading in.

Consider the important trading analysis

Irrespective of the type of a trader that you are, critical and important analysis on trading patterns and factors affecting trading of forexes is not to be ignored. Just a small bit of information may change the trading scales to either make profits or losses.

Even when a trader is pressed for time, never make a trade on a pair of currencies without thoroughly evaluating them to avoid regretting later. For the long-term traders, an important analysis is to trigger you to make a change in the currency pairs for a profitable trade. Make use of the little time, if you are a swing trader, and do a proper analysis on the currencies before putting your money at stake for a loss. Many traders have failed to do so where their efforts to pairing profitable currencies came to naught.

Unplug from distractions when analyzing trading patterns

Distractions such as social media, the TV, background noise and many others are to be avoided when making an analysis. They tend to eat up a lot of time when it could have been spent wisely in analyzing and not miss out on an opportunity to make a trade that could have resulted in profits.

Unplug from social media for a while trading and shout out all the noise in your surrounding and fully concentrate on evaluating the currencies and making wise decisions on pairing them.

This saves a lot of time that otherwise could have been used in multitasking trading and other activities all the while not fully concentrating on each activity.

Come up with an information sorting strategy

There could be information overload on forex exchange and a lot of unnecessary news regarding the same that waste time for a trader goes through all that in a bid to make a successful pairing of currencies. There are also a lot of sites online that offer updates on forex trading and if a trader could subscribe to all of them, then all they could be doing is analyzing trading forexes and doing zero trading at all. Sort out the relevant information that only has effect on your currency pairs. It is also advisable to have reliable sites to get information from and not a lot of them or some bogus ones. This could have done by looking at the reviews that the sites have to prove whether that is useful or not. This is a strategy that could save a lot of time, especially to the new traders who jump into every forex trading bandwagon.

Sync your preferred trading time with profitable trading widows

In forex trading, timing goes a long way. It is everything. A trader should, therefore, come up with a strategy that ensures that their available time is also a profitable window to trade-in. It is not always that the free time you get and available to trade in will result in profits. Choose the most appropriate window and execute a trade. However, a trader should also be able to enjoy his or her free time and also at the same time make money through forex trading. This cannot be reiterated enough, sync your 'available time' with profitable trading windows.

Money Management

Money management strategies are important to a forex trader to ensure that the trades made are profitable and reduce the chance of a loss happening to the bare minimum. Forex can be a game of chance to the traders who are not so keen on learning about managing their money in this type of trade. New traders lose their money when pairing the wrong currencies, and even made the correct currencies by the trading patterns but at the wrong time. The rules on money management reduce the chances of having a negative account balance when it could have been avoided. Below are some of the important money management tips to consider when trading currencies to maximize profits.

Avoid overexcitement of the forex market

This I mainly applicable to the new traders who get overexcited on the trading patterns and tend to trade currencies in a rush with no proper analyzation of the currencies and the market, thereby leading to huge losses.

This should be avoided where the habit can turn out to be more of a game of chance or betting rather than wise trading. You don't have to make a new trade when an opening presents itself every hour. It can prove to a fateful and a damning idea where the profits made and accumulated may be lost in an attempt to reach for more. Don't be afraid to lie low for days when waiting for an opportune time to make a good trade that may have huge profits. Being antsy for quick money and chasing the forex market will most of the times result in losses.

Most assuredly it will. Analyze the market, an opening for a profitable trade will surely come. A trade made in an overexcitement of the market will not equate that made after a careful analysis of the trading patterns. Very few trades will be lost when this strategy is put into employ, especially to the new traders. No opportunities to trade and make profits, then no trade at all, a philosophy that should be a guide in making decisions in the forex market.

Overexcitement for the market can also be displayed by opening a lot of trades in a short period of time, which may work against you should the tables turned.

This habit, coupled with other equally poor money management strategies in forex trading, has left traders' accounts on the negative balance, wiping off a lot of profits. Let several necessary trades work for you.

Take caution to trade on leverage

Leverage might be a great way to make money, double money, as is the thought of many new traders. This is however not the way leverage tends to work. It may turn against your trade wiping all your profits. While on one hand, large leverage might increase your money when one pair of currency is making profits, it can also create losses in a very quick way. A trader has to look into ways how they can protect their startup capital before making huge profits on the same capital. Leverage can either work for the good or work for the worst where your money in trading forex is concerned. It is therefore advisable in choosing the level of leverage to trade in, putting in mind that it may go either way and when it doesn't work, the losses are steep, especially on large levels of leverage. Being a cautious trader, you'll look into the balance that you have in your account before making the decision on the level of leverage you'll have on your capital. Other factors to put into consideration are such as the risk per trade and the stop loss distance. You have to look at how fast the system can respond to the cut of loss before running a lot of losses. When considering the risk per trade, carefully analyze whether the trade you are about to make will profitable and whether it is worth your money, or whether there is a change of a loss occurring, especially when you have a high level of leverage on your money.

Cut the trade when running a loss, keep the trade when gaining

Most of the new traders do not know when to cut the trade when they are on a streak of running losses. Not all trades making losses will reversibly start to make profits and the losses made will be converted to profits. In some cases, this is not what happens. It is advisable to keep the profits and let the cut loose of the losses by doing away with the trade that may wipe off your account. On the other hand, when your trade is making gains and profits, let it run. Let the profits accumulate. Some traders, in fear of the volatility of the market, often close trades that are making profits while fearing that there will be a reversal on the trade and losses will start to be made. This can happen when trades making profits have run for a long time and traders become skeptical. Traders who've been around for a long time have the philosophy of letting the winning trades run and not leaving losing trades open. This is a money management strategy that is very crucial. Traders who are mainly unprofessional and inexperienced fall mainly on leaving the losing trades open. The reason behind it may be because of greed for more money. This works against traders in many cases. Fear, on the other hand, motivates the traders who cut the trades that are making profits. They miss out on many opportunities to make a lot of money from the trades they closed. On this, it is also of great import to be cautious when making a decision on which trade to close and which trade to leave open. It is the forex market, after all, it is volatile as it is. Use the information available for proper analysis and make informed decisions.

CHAPTER 19:

How Is Forex Trading Beneficial to the Financial Market?

More than a hundred years ago, institutional traders and large banks were the only entities that had the means to access Forex markets. Today, the recent technological advancements and the wide use of IoT devices have enabled small traders to take advantage of the various benefits of the foreign exchange market. Similar to NASDAQ, online trading platforms allow small traders to buy and sell currencies on the market.

Forex and the World

Most of the currencies of the world are on a flexible exchange rate. This means that the value of a currency of a particular country fluctuates in response to the latest trends and events that are related to the foreign exchange market.

A floating currency is the exact opposite e of a fixed currency. The value of the latter depends on material goods, another currency, or a currency basket—a portfolio of selected currencies with different weightings. Commonly, governments used the currency basket to reduce the risk of currency fluctuation

In the modern world, the most widely used currencies are floating. These include the Swiss franc, the Indian rupee, the euro, the pound sterling, the Japanese yen, the Australian dollar, and the US dollar. Still. Even with floating currencies, central banks often participate in the foreign exchange market to influence the value of fluctuating exchange rates.

Worldwide, most nations have central banks. About seventy-five percent of the central bank assets are controlled by China, Japan, the US, and the countries in the Eurozone. A central bank is a national bank. It provides banking and financial services for its country's government and banking system. It also implements the government's monetary policy and currency issuance.

The Canadian dollar closely resembles an untainted floating currency. The central bank of Canada hasn't interfered with its value since 1998. The USD runs second to the CAD since the US made little change to its FX reserves. Forex reserves are assets and cash held by a central bank or similar monetary authority. The primary purposes of such organizations are to balance payments of the country, to maintain confidence in financial markets, and to influence the Forex rate of its currency.

Contrastingly, Japan and the United Kingdom intervene a lot. Japan is known for its systematic currency devaluation, and more recently, North Korea also devalued their won to curb inflation rates.

One of the largest and most influential macro-economic themes that affected automation suppliers was the devaluation of Japan's currency. Both Japan and China are manufacturing economies. As stated earlier, exports become cheaper when the currency of a country is devalued. This increases the number of local jobs since tourists and that country's citizens use the local currency pay for local products. This improves the economy, curbs inflation, and increases demand. When demand is high, more job opportunities are available for the people.

In 1973, the Smithsonian Agreement collapsed, and most of the currencies around the world followed suit. Yet, some countries, like the Gulf States, fixed their currency to another currency's value. This, however, is associated with a slower growth rate. With a floating currency, targets, except for the exchange rate, are utilized to implement monetary policy.

Today, it's considered that the currencies all over the world are on a floating rate of exchange. They're always traded in pairs, such as Dollar/Yen, Euro/Dollar, etc. Approximately eighty-five percent of worldwide daily transactions involve Forex trading of major currencies.

Four currency pairs are often utilized for investment purposes. They are the following: US dollar against Japanese yen, Euro against the US, US dollar against the Swiss franc, and British pound against the US dollar. In the trading market, they look like the following: USD/JPY, GBP/USD, USD/CHF, and EUR/USD.

If one currency will appreciate against another, it's recommended to exchange the quote currency for the base currency. By doing so, you can stay in it. In general terms, appreciation is the increase in an asset's value over time. In a floating rate exchange system, the changes in the value are based on demand and supply in the FX market. Appreciation is linked directly to demand. If the value goes up (appreciates), the demand for the currency rises as well.

If your predictions are right, you can initiate the opposite deal. This is done to exchange the first currency for the other and then collecting the profits from it.

Dealers at forex brokerage companies perform transactions on the FX market. Forex is integral to the world market. Hence, while you sleep in your bed, the dealers in the Eurozone are trading currencies with their American counterparts.

Clients can place stop-loss and take-profit orders with brokers. Brokers perform overnight executions. Price movements on the foreign exchange market are smooth. Unlike in the stock market, they don't have gaps every morning. New investors can exit and enter positions without encountering issues because the daily turnover on the Forex market is approximately USD 1.2 trillion.

In truth, the FX market never ceases to stop. The foreign exchange market is the oldest and largest financial market worldwide. When you compare the Forex market with others, you'll see that the market for currency futures only comprises one percent of all Forex transactions. Unlike the stock and futures market, currency trading is decentralized. This means that it isn't centered on any exchange. Currency trading moves from major financial centers of the United States to Europe, Australia, and New Zealand, to Europe, and back to the US. It's a sort of a cycling trading game. To reiterate, large financial institutions and major currency dealers were the only ones to take advantage of the Forex market's liquidity and the amazing trending nature of the world's primary currency pairs. However, today, Forex brokers can break down larger-sized inter-bank units. Because of this, they can offer total beginners and small traders' opportunities to trade in small increments.

Brokers and trading platforms offer small-to-medium companies and individual spectators' options for trading at the same rates and price movements. Two decades ago, only big players like banks dominated the Forex market.

How Can Banks Intervene with Forex Rates?

Central banks have the power to influence foreign exchange rates. The member countries of the European Union (EU) agreed to maintain a band around target exchange rates. When necessary, they will implement this monetary policy through intervention in Forex markets. Even without exchange rate commitments, Japan and the United States often intervene in global FX markets in order to stabilize the value of their domestic currency. Central banks can use a "foreign exchange intervention" as a monetary policy device. When a central bank influences a currency's funds transfer rate, they do so use their asset reserves or their authority to generate banknotes and coinage.

More often than not, central banks in developing countries intervene in Forex markets so that they could build reserves for themselves. Or, they provide for another country's national banks to stabilize exchange rates. Stabilization invites traders to place investments on a particular nation or Forex market. It makes them feel comfortable with the exchanges that are going to transpire on the marketplace. Currency stabilization requires both long-term and short-term interventions. Destabilizing effects may come from both non-market or market forces.

When a central financial institution increases the amount of money circulating within an economy, extra care is needed to reduce its inadvertent effects like hyperinflation.

The efficacy of a Forex intervention relies heavily on how the organization central to the policy mitigates the consequences of the intervention.

In implementing an intervention, central banks face three challenges:

1. The number of reserve assets of a country
2. The economic issues faced by the government
3. The volatile market conditions of the Forex exchanges associated with the nation

Often, after the execution of monetary policies, a corrective intervention may be required. This is done to fix and mitigate the consequences and issues that resulted from the initial intervention of the central bank.

Forex Intercessions Come in Two Types:

1. The government or central agency assesses its currency

When the financial organization determines that the value of the domestic currency is too high for the economies of other countries, especially those that import their products or goods, the central bank of the country in question or another nation will definitely intervene. Their fiat currency should be affordable for their major consumers.

Hence, even though the majority of the world's currencies are floating, there are instances wherein a central agency needs to control or bolster the value of their currency. The only currency that can be considered pure, in terms of being tarnished with repeated interventions, is the CAD. As stated before, the Canadian government had not intervened with the exchange rate of their legal tender in the last forty years.

For example, from the end of Q3 2011 to the start of Q1 2015, the Swiss National Bank (SNB) set a minimum exchange rate between the Euro and Swiss Franc. This prevented the Swiss franc from increasing beyond a level at which their major importers couldn't afford their Swiss goods.

For more than three years, this proved to be advantageous for Switzerland and its importers. However, the Swiss National Bank determined that it must let the Swiss Franc to freely float. Without warning other countries, they released the minimum exchange rate.

2. The intervention is a short-term response to an economic or political event

Often, an event can make a country's currency move in a specific direction over a short period. In this case, a central bank will try to reduce the market's volatility and provide liquidity through intervention.

After the SNB allowed their currency to stay afloat, the Swiss franc decreased in value by approximately twenty-five percent. After this, the SNB implemented a corrective intervention to mitigate the volatility.

On paper, Forex interventions can sometimes be risky. Set monetary policies can even undermine the credibility of a bank when it can't maintain stability.

Defending the domestic currency from speculators was the cause of the economic crisis in Mexico in 1994. A similar event also happened in Thailand, which sparked the 1997 Asian Financial Crisis.

CHAPTER 20:

Pips and What You Need to Know About Them

What Is A Pip?

When you get into the foreign exchange circle, chances are you will encounter the word pip countless times as you begin your journey through the currency trading market. So, what is a pip, and why is it so important in this trade?

In foreign exchange (Forex), pip is the 'point in percentage'. When a currency pair is traded, the pip is what is used to detect losses and gains.

A pip is seen as the basic unit in the Forex market and therefore, for you to be successful in this trade, you will need to understand it. In most currencies, it is represented by the last figure in four decimal places. 0.0003. The three here is the pip. Therefore, if an exchange rate of the USD to say KSHS is 1 USD = 102.1675, the 5 at the end is the pip.

For example, the US Dollar, probably them the most stable currency in the world and therefore, the currency onto which others are held up against, is often measured on a pip of 0.0001.

There are notable exceptions though, with the Japanese Yen being the most common.

The USD pip point against the JPY is often to three decimal places; therefore, the pip is 0.001.

What is The Function of the Pip?

Now, we have stated above that the pip is a basic unit of foreign exchange and therefore, is one of the things you will need to be aware of as you enter the currency trading market. But right now, the question you ask 'Why is the pip and understanding it important?'

Due to fluctuations in the Forex market, the pip was developed to be able to handle the shifts in the exchange rates. Had it been a larger figure, say well into the ones and tens units of measurement, it would greatly affect not just prices in the Forex market, but it would have the potential to cause far-reaching effects, like changes in prices in commodities in the consumer market. if the pip was said, 1, an increase of two would be a huge shift, with the potential to shift economies.

Therefore, by having the pip value low in the decimal figure, they were able to develop a mechanism that would ensure more stability during fluctuations, even though, as we will discover further down the article, it still is a figure that can quickly grow into huge amounts. So, let's look at some of the terms we could encounter in this field.

Ask Price, Bid Price, and Spread: Term You Should Be Familiar With

Once you set foot in the Forex trading world, you will come across several terminologies, and today, right here, we look at some of the most important ones used.

Let's say you want to sell a currency pair. The price you put forth is what we will define as the 'ask' price as the price. The asking price is, then, the price that you would give when buying a currency pair. It is slightly higher than the market price.

The price that you can sell a currency pair is called the bid price. It is often the price put on display in banks and Forex halls. You will find that this bid price is lower than the market price, which will ensure that whoever buys from you sells it at the market price so as to get a profit.

Then, we have spread. If, say, the bid price is 1.9786 and the asking price is 1.9792, the difference of 6 pips (1.9792 - 1.9786) is the spread. So, we can look at spread as the pip difference between a bid and ask price.

In foreign exchange, it is important to note that Forex happens with two pairs of currencies, where one sells one to buy another. They are called currency pairs

For example, if you have the GBP (Great Britain Pound) and wants to change it with the USD, this will be called trading the USD/GBP pair. Therefore, when you give your GBP to get the USD, you will be selling the GBP and buying the USD.

Popular Currency Pairs in Trading

So, now you think, in order to make the right risks, what popular currency pairs do I need to be aware of?

Popular currency pairs will often be from more developed countries. This is because, since they have more stable economies, their currencies are subjected to less volatility and manipulation due to very small pip values between their exchange rates. They tend to also have more political stability, thus making their markets more certain, and thus, trading in their currencies less risky than others. You will then find that these currencies become the most traded and often, the pairing of one stable currency to another becomes more popular and less risky. But, as it is said, in the Forex business, the risk is the name of the game.

Examples of some of the most popular currency pairs are GBP/USD (British Pound and the US Dollar, USD/JPY (The US Dollar and the Japanese Yen), EUR/USD

As seen from above, the US Dollar is seen to be the most stable, occurring in most of the common currency pair. It is the most stable currency in the world, which is why you can conduct business using US Dollars in pretty much any country in the world. It often has a low spread when traded with others hence its popularity. However, other common pairs could include GBP/JPY, EUR/GBP. These are referred to as Cross currencies, so defined because they do not feature the USD.

Then, there are the so-called exotic pairs. This is the currency pairs between the developing world, as they are colloquially known. Because of their instability, they are more volatile and therefore, are often considered riskier to trade. This is also influenced by the political temperatures, which often has wide implications in the market certainty/uncertainty. An example of this pair could be the USD/KSHS

How Do I Calculate Pips?

Now to the math.

To get the value of the pip, you will need to divide 1/10,000 or 0.0001 (the pip is calculated to the fourth decimal) by the exchange rate. As noted earlier, this is an exception when you are trading the USD, or the EUR with the Japanese Yen, which registers pips with 2 decimal place, that is 0.01.

Pip Value

So, hypothetically speaking, let's say you have the USD/GBP currency pair and you get a quote 0.7754. This means 1 USD will get you 0.7754 GBP. A one pip increase - 0.7755 - would mean that 1 USD will then become more valuable as it will earn you a bit more GBPs.

If, say, you then decide to buy 2000 GBPs with US Dollars, you will then first divide the USD/GBP exchange rate then multiply by the number of Euros you want to buy.

So, it will be [1/0.7754] x 2000 = 2579.31. The price paid will be 2579.31.

If there is a one pip increase in the exchange rate - to 0.7755 - then the calculation would be

[1/0.7755] x 2000 = 2578.98.

Therefore, the pip value between the currencies would be 2579.31 - 2578.98 = USD 0.33.

The more one puts in the trading, the higher the pip value.

Pipettes; a Further Figure

Further down the figures, we get the pipette. Pipettes allow spreading to happen over an even wider area, meaning that it further reduces the risks that come with Forex trading. This is measured as 1/10th of a pip. In most normal pair currencies, it is measured as the fifth number after the decimal place, but when it comes to the Japanese Yen against the dollar, it is represented as third decimal place. Usually, it is displayed in superscript format.

For example, in 1 USD = 0.77576 GBP, the 6 at the end is the pipette.

Pips and Profits: What Affects Your Gains/Losses?

As stated above, the movement of the currency pair determines whether you make gains or losses.

So, for example, if you want to buy into the USD/EUR pair. If the prices of the Euro goes up when you sell, you profit from the increase. So, say you bought Euros for 1.1843 and then, when you sell, the market price is at 1.1896, your profit will be the 53 pips on the trade.

Relatively speaking, the difference is small. But the Forex market is a big deal, often determining economies of entire countries and the market prices. Gains and losses add up quickly, thus, meaning that the slightest change can have a high impact and have far-reaching consequences. Small changes will often result in small fluctuations which, when considered over time and consistently, will have bigger consequences. Thus, while it may be a small figure to the untrained eye, a seasoned trader knows the value of a pip. Therefore, so should you.

Why Is It Important To Understand Pip

Understanding pips and pip values are important before you put your money into Forex trading. Among the benefits are;

To Follow the Gains/losses

Seasoned traders often gain the advantage by knowing how the fluctuations of pip values will influence their profit/losses.

Understanding the change in pip value helps you as a trader strategies on which deals will be worth putting your stakes.

To Identify Strong Currency Pairs

When you understand the pip values, you will better be able to access the currency pairs in the market, follow through those that combine well and trade favorably and thus, know where to place your risks.

As we have learned above, a small pip change can have wide implications and this could quickly add up to either gains or losses.

Therefore, you will have an understanding of this when you look at the currency pairs.

Leverage

Leverage provides you with the ability to trade with amounts of money that are more than you have on your deposits. If the leverage is, say 30, this will mean that, for every one dollar you have in your deposit, for example, you will control 30 in the Forex market, thus, increasing chances of a huge profit.

Therefore, understanding the pip values will allow you better gauge the risks that are involved in the trading you are about to undertake and choose reasonable leverage sizes that won't dent your pockets in the event of losses.

CHAPTER 21:

Mistakes and Tips for Beginners in Forex Trading

The forex market due to its low restriction makes the market one of the most available market in the world. With an internet connection, phone or computer, and some few dollars, you can begin trading in the market. However, because of its free accessibility does not mean it is easy to make huge returns.

Forex Mistakes

Mistakes in forex are unavoidable but there are always remedies to deal with such a situation. Before you consider plunging into trading, it is important to consider the following mistakes and do everything possible to avoid them in the future. Most people are persuaded to venture into forex trading with fantasies of getting rich overnight.

Undeniably, the opportunities in the forex market are innumerable for you to make money and live the lifestyle you want. Notwithstanding, the forex road is not an easy road to travel because it is full of bumps. If there is anything, I can assure you as a beginner is that you will struggle for various reasons including having a poor forex foundation, poor trading structure, and impatience.

Tips for Trading Forex

Learning to trade successfully in the forex market is quite problematical for new traders. Most traders have the mindset of getting rich overnight, which is not something realistic. Forex trading can be prodigious particularly if you are a beginner and do not know the rules guiding the market. These tips will help you in your trading journey as a beginner. It is always advisable not to forget the basics because without them you will struggle in the market.

Pick Your Broker Cleverly

If you can choose the right broker, then you are halfway done in the forex market. Before choosing any broker, it is important for you to review various brokers. Ensure to seek recommendations from professional traders and make your own research because some traders will recommend a particular broker because of their affiliate programs. Take your time as we have various fake brokers looking for traders like you to ripe off. Do not be moved by mouthwatering deals, rather look for an authorized broker with years of accomplishment.

Develop Your Strategy

A list of tips on forex trading is not complete without mentioning strategy. As a beginner, you need to create your own trading strategy that works for you. Every trader should know what to expect and get from the market. You should set a definite goal because it will help discipline yourself when trading.

Learn Slowly

Forex is not something you learn and stop over time. Every new skill requires consistent learning to grasp the basics. Additionally, you do not have to rush your learning process. Take your time slowly and begin by investing a little amount of money. Remember that slow and steady will win the race as a beginner.

Control Your Emotions

If you allow your emotions to guide you when trading, you will regret it later. I am not telling you that it is easy but you can control it. You need to stay rational in order to make wise choices during trading. If you let your emotions to rule over you, you are bound to expose yourself to pointless risks. Forex trading is risky but you can control the level of risk that can happen.

Do Not Trade If You Are Under Stress

Hardly can you see someone who concentrates optimally when under stress. Traders who decide to do that will surely make an irrational decision, which will cost them money. Therefore, before thinking of trading, ensure to identify anything that will cause stress and eliminate them before it eliminates your forex account (do not mind me I am just joking but there is a sense to it). If you had a stressful day and still had to trade, consider taking a deep breath while allowing your mind to focus on what you are about to do. You can overcome stress in various ways such as exercising, sleeping, and listening to music, hanging out with friends. Whatever the situation is, find a solution to your stress and manage it effectively.

Never Stop Practicing

Do not neglect this tip because it is crucial to your success or failure as a forex trader. Hardly can you succeed on your first encounter in the forex market. Therefore, when you make your first mistake, do not relent because, with consistent practicing, you will be among the top traders. However, you have the adventure of using a demo account to perfect your skill.

Risk Is Part of The Game

If you are not ready to risk, you are not ready for the forex market. Most brokers will advise you that trading is risky and you should accept that fact. If you think that in forex you are going to have a sweet ride, then you need a reality check. Additionally, I have seen mouthwatering advertisements promising you the "unpromising." Well, you should be realistic about your goals and strategies.

Patience is Priceless

Do you remember the old adage? "True success is never instantaneous." That holds true in the forex market. It is the product of consistent planning and work, which many beginners tend to overlook. There is no easy path to making a profit in the market. Let patience have her way in you.

Upgrade Your Knowledge Continuously

The more you trade, the newer things you learn. Improve your knowledge by looking at trends, analyzing news, and financial processes. Furthermore, do not neglect the fundamental basis you have learned. Significantly, you should study, practice, and continue this routine. A knife gets dull when it is left idle. Sharpen your trading skill with continuous learning and practicing.

Take Breaks

All work and no play make Jack a dull student. You can take routine breaks especially when you are under stress. For those glued to multiple computer winds to analyze data from various source, it is important to take a break as you may feel pressured.

Understand the Charts

You will trade in various markets and these require different information to analyze each trade. We have numerous tools you can use to make your trading easier. However, charts are time efficient and serve as the best option for beginners. You should not know them only; you should learn how to read and use them to your advantage.

Incorporate stop-losses in your trades

Setting stop-loss for trade is an efficient strategy to use when trading. With stop-loss, you minimize your risk and escape any trade that goes haywire. Additionally, avoid greediness by setting the maximum profit and loss range. Once you hit your target, you should avoid the trap of placing another trade.

CHAPTER 22:

How to Make Money with Forex Trading to Create Passive Income

According to experts in the field of Forex Trading, it is possible to create a passive income through this form of financial trading. However, before jumping headlong into this type of financial trading, prospective traders need to ask themselves whether it is suitable for them, in addition to learning as much as possible about this line of business.

A passive income is the income stream traders or investors get at regular intervals and require little or no effort on their part to maintain it. Some of the common types of passive income include dividends from stock owned in a listed corporation, rental income, and interest income from bonds.

Other less common forms of passive income include royalties from a music record or publishing a book, or dividends from a non-listed company run by a family member or friend. Passive income may also arise from a new business model or income from a multi-level marketing network, where the income originates from other people's activities.

Some internet marketers, such as affiliate marketers, also receive passive income from internet traffic that continues to stream in from blogs they posted a long time ago. Nowadays, traders can make a passive income through the forex market.

In fact, one does not have to participate directly in the trading process or have tons of experience in this field of business. Forex traders can earn a passive income from this form of financial trading in several ways, with some requiring more work or input from the trader. Some of these include:

Forex Signals

These are short messages new traders can use to determine the best currency to trade and the right time to trade. Traders can receive important trading information through email, text messages, or any other type of communication, including social media platforms such as TX forums, Twitter, and other leading financial trading platforms.

These signals or messages are usually brief snippets of information, which instruct users to take specific actions, such as purchasing EUR/USD at a certain price. Sometimes, these signals feature various types of orders, such as a market order, pending order, or limit order. There are tons of sites that teach traders how to read and understand forex signals.

These signals can also be premium or free, with the former leading to better trades. Many providers of forex signals freely send important trading information to investors to boost their reputation in the financial trading industry. Forex signals are also great for people who want to earn a passive income trading options but do not have the time or opportunity to learn much about Forex Trading.

However, it is important to perform adequate research into providers of forex signals to avoid losing money. Forex traders, however, should approach these signals with utmost caution to make a good passive income.

Forex Robots

One of the best ways to make a passive income from the forex market is using a tool known as a forex robot, which performs automated trades on a trader's behalf. Once traders set up these forex robots, they do not have to do much else; however, they should keep an eye on the trades the forex robots are making for them.

To get started, traders need to perform adequate research into the software available for forex robots. They need to choose software that will meet their needs, in addition to being reliable when it comes to executing the right forex trades. After setting up this software, it will make forex trades based on preset signals.

In addition, it will use its acquired knowledge to purchase or sell at specific times, earning users a passive income in the process. However, it is important to understand that not all forex robots make passive income for investors as claimed. In the same way that a human can make a losing trade, a forex robot can also make the same mistake.

It is also important to understand that many so-called forex robots are frauds, which is why respected news platforms such as the Wall Street Journal and Forbes refuse to promote or advertise them. Unfortunately, this is particularly true when it comes to free forex robots. Therefore, new forex traders should analyze testimonials and reviews carefully before entrusting their investment to a forex robot.

Fortunately, several leading sites focus on reviewing different trading platforms. These sites try to give an honest opinion of different investment platforms and outline all the benefits and limitations of each platform. They also offer a detailed analysis of how these platforms work and how traders can get started on them, which is especially helpful to new traders.

Social Trading

The social trading network works in the same way as a social networking platform. Instead of sharing selfies or pictures of pets playing the piano, however, social traders share important information about forex or financial trades. This allows others to copy them and make passive income as well.

New forex traders simply need experienced traders they trust and copy their trading strategies to make money. In addition to making a passive income, they will also learn when, why, and how successful traders make their trading moves, which will give them more insight and understanding into the forex industry.

However, finding traders, they can trust and emulate is not as easy as it may sound. New traders need to set aside adequate time to perform thorough research into different social trading platforms, in addition to learning more about forex traders they want to work with and copy.

In certain situations, they might need to spend some money on the trader whose trading strategies they copy. However, this commission is negligible and not a big concern for new traders who want to make a passive income. Forex Trading is something that most people looking for ways to make some extra cash look into.

However, most of them do not know where to start. This discussion provides three great ideas for Forex Trading beginners to consider. Each of the options above requires a different investment in terms of time and effort. The most important thing to remember is that beginners should perform adequate research before picking a trading platform or strategy to use.

Nowadays, Forex Trading is one of the best ways for people to make a passive income working online. Millions of traders are earning a passive or active income every day through Forex Trading. This line of business is just like any other online money-making concept, but its profit potential is unrivaled. With modern technological advances and the availability of detailed information, anyone can make a passive income through Forex Trading.

CHAPTER 23:

Compound Interest And Forex

Earning more means being paid more. We usually think that others should pay us more if we want to make more money, but this is not always true. We can earn more even if we pay ourselves more, and not the others.

This is a fundamental principle underlying the financial success, first disclosed in 1926 by George Samuel Clason through his book entitled The Richest Man in Babylon, a great motivational classic.

The principle states that part of what you earn must be maintained. Putting aside at least 10% of what you earn—and making that money inaccessible to ordinary expenses and possibly even extraordinary expenses—you can increase this amount exponentially over time. Considering any investments, thanks to the power of the compound investment, the amount saved or invested over the years can become important. In fact, many people can earn more and build their assets by paying themselves first. It is a true and effective principle today as it was in 1926.

Yet, as this 10% formula is easy, people are unwilling to listen to it and apply it. This is because you are usually looking for tricks to get rich quickly, and you do not have a medium to long-term vision. On the other hand, having a long-term investment plan is a solid foundation for building one's own economic stability. And you can start earning more by paying yourself first from today. The earlier you start, the quicker you will build your financial success.

Using The Power Of Compound Interest

To earn more, you can take advantage of the compound interest. Here's how it works: if you invest €1,000 at a 5% interest, you will earn €50 of interest, and at the end of the first year, you will have a total investment of €1,050. If you leave both the initial investment and the interest earned on the current account, you will receive a 5% interest the following year over €1,050, or €52.50. In the third year, you will earn 5% out of 1,102.50, and so on. At this rate, within 15-30 years your money will turn into an amount well above the sum invested initially. But precisely how much does the invested capital grow? Luca Pacioli explained it in the 15th century: any capital doubles in some years equal to 72 divided by the interest rate. Returning to our example: if the interest is at 5% per year, we divide 72 by 5; which makes 14.4 (i.e., in 14 years and 4 months the initial capital doubles). The sooner you start, the bigger the result will be, as you will have more time for the interest you capitalize on produce its powerful magic. Start now to save and invest for your future, even if you do not have a large sum. You do not need to have an extra sum of money. You can start with any amount and grow it over time.

The Secret Of Paying Of Yourself First

If you want to earn more money by paying yourself first, you have to make savings and investment a central part of your financial management, just like the mortgage payment. Get accustomed to saving a fixed percentage (at least 10%) of your monthly income and investing it in special savings account that you decide not to touch. Ideally, this step would be automatic, such as a fixed monthly deduction on your paycheck. The automation will ensure that you will not have to rely on your self-discipline and your ability to save will not be affected by your mood from domestic emergencies or otherwise. Continue to increase that account until you have saved enough to invest the sum accumulated in bonds, in a mutual fund or real estate (spending money on rent without building any assets is really a waste). Let your investments build your assets over time and try to live with what remains after you have paid yourself. If you want to spend, try to earn more to afford it. But never put your hands on your savings to finance a more ambitious lifestyle. The ideal would be for your investments to grow to the point where you could live with interest, if necessary. Only then will you really be financially autonomous and free.

If you want to earn more, you need to create assets, not liabilities. Rather than spending all the money you earn by enriching someone else, invest in assets that produce other income (stocks, bonds, real estate, gold, etc.). When your money starts to grow, educate yourself further about the best way to invest your money. Stay informed about news about investment opportunities and remember to protect what is yours through a good insurance policy. Do not blindly trust who will manage your money, but always try to improve your financial education. This will make you a financially prepared person ready to get rich. Once you understand this, money will follow.

What is compound interest? Not everyone may know how to respond immediately to this question. If everyone knows what the simple interest is (i.e., the one that withdraws at the end of the agreed time unit), fewer are those who know what the compound interest is, how it works, and, most importantly, how to take advantage of it.

The example of a bank account is enlightening.

If on 1 January, I have a net rate of 1% on my account, at the end of the year I have €101. A euro more is added to the capital and, if the conditions do not change, at the end of the second year, I will not have €102, but €102 and a cent where the cent represents 1% of the euro accumulated after the first year.

So far, everything is clear, but most of us cannot calculate the compound interest of investment and tend to treat it as simple interest. This is due to its slow start, that, especially with small capital, tends to be treated as "irrelevant". However, there is nothing more wrong that an investor could do.

If, for example, after 5 years of investment, my capital of €100 is now €140, we are led to believe that the interest was 8% per year.

This is incorrect because, in doing so, we do not take into account that at the end of each period the interest accumulate has gone to increase capital. If the interest had really been 8%, composing the 5 years we would have had

Initial capital: €100

- 1st year: €108
- 2nd year: €116.64
- 3rd year: €125.97
- 4th year: €136.04
- 5th year: €146.93

The difference (€6.93) represents almost 7% of the total. As you can see, it is easy to take dazzle (and worse, even "suffer", if for some reason we are offered a simple interest for a compound interest).

The Maths Behind Compound Interest: An Easy Example

Suppose we have an initial capital of €1,000. The capital yields a Y% interest and this interest is calculated on an annual basis.

What will be the value of the investment after X years?

The calculation formula is as follows:

(1) $IV = CP (1 + Y) \wedge X$

IV is the value of the investment after X years, while CP is the initial capital. Y is expressed as a percentage, i.e. 0.04 indicates 4%. The symbol ^ is the symbol of elevation to power.

The inverse calculation tends to find the Y interest of an investment that now (net of inflation) is worth IV against a CP capital invested X periods (years) ago. The formula is:

(2) Y = (IV / CP) ^ (1 / X) - 1

Suppose that, after inflation, €1,000 invested 5 years ago are now worth €1,400, you immediately have that the yield was 6.96%.

Let's take a look at another example:

Marie has just taken the salary and can finally buy the air conditioner she needs.

But her friend Julie calls her to tell her that she has an urgent need that she cannot cope with immediately and asks her to borrow €1,000.

Marie is undecided because this would mean waiting another month before she can make her purchase.

To resolve the issue, the two girls agree on the loan provided that Julie returns the money to Mary with a 5% interest (the numbers are purely random for the example).

In this way, Marie has a greater incentive to have to delay her purchase.

When Julie returns the sum loaned, she will receive €1,050 instead of €1,000.

The following month, Marie can buy the air conditioner and, to celebrate, use the accumulated interest (€50) to go out to dinner with her boyfriend.

In short, in the end, this recognition for the delayed use was not bad!

Now that we understand the concept behind the rate of interest, it is good to enter a little more in detail and make some distinctions.

In this regard, we can divide the interest rate into two broad categories:

1. The simple interest
2. The compound interest

Simple Interest:

Let's go back to the previous example.

At the end of the period, Julie returns the money plus the interest to Mary. Soon after, however, the girl asks the same amount again to buy a new refrigerator, as the old one suddenly broke.

Marie agrees to lend the money back to her friend.

The following month, Julie firmed up her debt plus new interests, again for a total of €1,050.

Now, Marie is with her initial capital, plus €100 in interest, for a total of €1,100.

Interest is defined as simple when, once it has matured on the underlying capital, it does not generate further interest.

In our example, we note that the first €50 was not added to the capital loaned the second time.

Compound Interest:

Change of scenery.

Julie asks Marie to lend her €1,000 with the promise to return them in two years.

Mary agrees, as long as Julie accepts a compound interest on the mature borrowed capital.

In this case, Julie will not have to pay the interest immediately at the end of the 1st year but will add the € 50 interest in the capital, which will accumulate 5% in the 2nd year.

At the end of the agreed period, Julie must therefore return:

1. €1,000 capital
2. €50 interest for the first year (€1,000 + 5%)
3. €52.50 interest for the second year (€1.050 + 5%)

The total capital to be returned to Mary is, therefore, € 1,102.50.

Here we have materialized € 2.50 more than the previous example, due to the compound interest.

The interest is defined as compound when, once it has matured on the underlying capital, it is added to the latter and contributes to generating further increased interest in the future.

Do you understand why the compound interest is your new best friend?

When you deposit your money in the bank account you are doing as Marie, that is, you are "lending" your money to the bank, which uses them to perform its credit function and lend it to people and businesses.

CHAPTER 24:

The Resistance Trading Strategy

The support and resistance that we talked about before can be used to help you come up with the perfect trading strategy as well. In fact, this can be a great way to help you do well with purchasing securities at the right time and to reduce your costs and increase your profits.

In these strategies, the support is going to be the price level you will purchase. This price level is going to be very strong, and it is about to reverse or interrupt the downtrend and will go back up soon. When the downward trend hits the support level, it is likely to bounce again, and the price will rise. If you purchase the security when it is almost to the support, you will receive the lowest price for the security at that time.

Then there is the resistance. This is going to be the opposite of the support. This is going to occur where the price level is so strong that it is going to reverse the uptrend and start going down. When the uptrends start to get near this level, the trend will likely stop, and then it will go down. You will want to sell the security as close to this resistance level to increase your profits as much as possible.

The resistance and the support are going to change daily. But sometimes it is difficult to find the line as clearly as others. The price movement of the security may be really volatile at some points of the day. And then there may be full days where you won't be able to create either the support line, the resistance line, or either of them. If you can't create the line, it may be better to pick out a different strategy. But if you can start your day looking at the charts and can draw some strong support or resistance lines, then this is the strategy that you should work with.

The good news is that there are various steps that you can work with on the charts that you gather for an asset. Bring those out, and use the steps below to help you draw your own support and resistance levels to help you work on your own trades:

- Often half dollars and whole dollars can be good support and resistance levels. This is especially true when you work on stocks under $10. If you can't find your support or your resistance lines, check here and see if your line would work there.

- When you make your own lines, you need to have the most recent data available. This ensures that you are getting the best information for that stock.

- The more that your line can touch the extreme price of the stock, the better option this line is for your support and resistance. If it is too far from this extreme point, then it is not going to have enough value to make it strong.

- Only look at any support or resistance lines that stay with the current price range. For example, if the stock's price is around $20 right now, you do not need to look at the region on the graph where the stock randomly jumped up to $40. This is not an area where the stock will probably go back to, so it doesn't make much sense to work from there.

- Many times, the support and resistance are not just one exact number. Often it is more of an area. If you come up with a support or resistance that is about $19.69, then you know that the movement is somewhere near that number, not exactly that number. You can usually estimate that the area will be somewhere between five to ten cents above or under that line.

- The price that you want to work from will need to have a clear bounce off that level. If you can't find that this price bounces at that level, then this is not a good support or resistance level for you to work with. Your levels need to be easy to notice and need to make sense for the charts you look at. If you have any questions about whether you picked the right one or not, it's not the right one.

As you are going through and creating these lines, you will find that it isn't always as simple as it seems. You want to take extra care to pick out the right spots for these lines, or you will make bad decisions with your trading. The good news is that the more you draw these lines and do the trades, the better you will get at doing it.

After you take the time to draw the lines on your charts, you can then make your own trading strategy, which is there to help you purchase or sell the securities you want, and the timing will be based on the lines you drew. The steps that you can take to make this kind of trading strategy to work after drawing your lines will include:

1. When you first get up in the morning, sit down and make a watchlist. Take a look at your charts and draw out the resistance and the support lines that go with the information you have. Use the steps above to help draw these lines.

2. Now you need to create your five-minute chart. Then spend some time watching the action of the price, watching how it responds to those lines. If you find that near the line there is a type of indecision candle, then this is the exact confirmation you are looking for to determine you picked the right line. Now is the time to get into the trade. Your goal here is to purchase your security as near to that support level as you can to reduce the risks but realize that it's unlikely you will get right on the line.

3. Once you enter the trade, you need to consider when you would like to withdraw from the trade to profit.

4. Keep the trade open for a bit, even after you have withdrawn. This makes it easier to hit the target you set for profit, or until you see that the security is forming with a new resistance and support level compared to what you originally drew.

5. You may decide that trading at a half position near your profit target. This allows them to move the stop when they want closer to the entry point to at least reach a break-even point.

6. If you are looking through the charts that you have, and you see that the support and resistance level have gone away, or they aren't obvious any longer, then it is time to close the trade and move on.

This is a very effective trading method to work with as a beginner. If it is done properly, and after you have some time to experiment withdrawing support and resistance levels, it is a great way to learn when to enter and exit the market. As long as you create the lines in the right places, and you know how to watch the market for the right entry and exit points, you will find that this strategy is really easy to work with.

Exchange Traded Funds (Etfs)

One of the most important trends of the financial world in the last two decades has been the rise of Exchange Traded Funds or ETFs. The first ETF like asset was introduced in 1989 and currently ETFs hold a total of more than 2.5 trillion dollars worldwide in over 1800 funds and the sector is still growing.

But what are they exactly? ETFs are "tracking" assets that follow certain groups (indices, sectors) of stocks bonds and other, mostly financial products. They are a bit like mutual funds but are traded like stocks on exchanges and also they are mostly passively managed— meaning that no fund manager is deciding on the allocation.

ETFs Versus Mutual Funds

According to numerous studies most fund managers fail to achieve the returns of stock indices that have a profound effect on asset allocation by money managers and individual investors alike. Whatever is the strategy or how sophisticated the manager is, 80% of funds underperform indices even without accounting for fees.

Passive investing is very cheap with ETFs, that's why a lot of investors choose index tracking ETFs and sector ETFs to get exposure to whole markets or particular sectors or industries rather than constructing a portfolio of individual stocks or buying a mutual fund. And it is not just the direct costs that are lower— taxing of gains is much more attractive in ETFs, although the difference is not the same in every country.

Still, the mutual fund industry is a magnitude bigger than the ETF industry as many big investment pools (such as insurance companies and pension funds) are simply not allowed to buy them as they are technically individual stocks.

Types Of ETFs

There is a wide variety of ETF choices that can help individual investors create a balanced portfolio throughout asset classes. To name a few, you can get exposure to the already mentioned

- Global stock indices
- Industry Sectors

And also

- Commodities
- Government Bonds
- Corporate Bonds
- Currencies
- Volatility
- Short exposure (inverse ETFs)

You can find comprehensive screeners for ETFs

Examples And Up-To-Date Tips

The biggest ETF, SPY, is naturally tracking the most traded stock index, the S&P 500. It's very low-cost structure (0.1%/year) and high liquidity makes it the top choice to get exposure to U.S. stocks for individuals and managers who are allowed to invest in or trade with it.

Bond and commodity ETFs might be very attractive in the current environment for several reasons. The market rout of the first few weeks of 2016 has been triggered by weakness in commodities that led to problems among high-yield ("junk") bonds. With ETFs, you can benefit from a possible rebound or more downside in those assets directly, and easily.

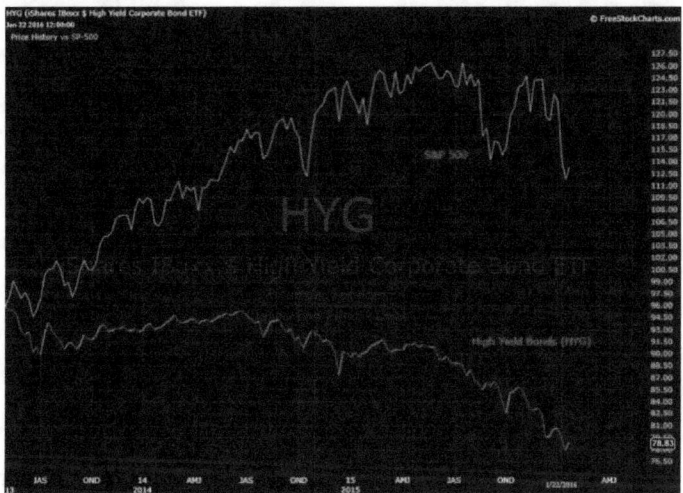

As you can see on the chart above, HYG, one of the biggest the high-yield bonds ETF, has been leading stocks lower lately and by buying or shorting it, you can play both sides of the current trend in a simple manner. The numerous commodity ETFs and inverse ETFs provide versatile ways of hedging, investing, or trading in these volatile times.

And whatever trends you think the future will bring these funds provide very effective choices to invest in your ideas and views without any middleman or extra commissions; so always kep ETFs in mind before deciding on asset allocation.

CHAPTER 25:

Practical Guide to the Trend-Line

To invest better in the financial markets, you must undoubtedly use the right indicators, so fortunately we can tell you that you have landed in the right place because here in our portal we want to offer professional advice and strategies for those who intend to take trading seriously and do it with technical analysis indicators.

We often hear that trading is simple, but this must not lead any trader to underestimate an activity that in all respects entrepreneurial and serious like trading, consequently you have to plan everything, have a solid foundation and do studies with dedication to achieve important results.

As you probably already know with trading you will not get results immediately especially if you do not perform a very detailed graphic analysis. We often see traders throwing their capital away for the simple fact of investing without any criteria and without using any tactics or strategy.

For completeness, we also say that many traders throw capital upside down because they choose the trading platform incorrectly.

The importance of the trend-line indicator

One of the simplest but effective ways to study the price movements on the markets and to use technical indicators and in particular the trend-lines, each indicator has its qualities but there are some more important and used than others all of them are used to read the past. The topicality of the market to foreshadow future price movements with the greatest possible precision, of course, this does not mean being able to predict the future of what will happen in the market. Still, the interesting thing is that you can reach an excellent degree of approximation.

This is why we strive to emphasize the importance of using indicators and that is why we choose to draw up such papers. By continuing to read, you can learn more about the use of trend-lines and how you can use them in investing on the markets, whether it is forex, stocks, indices or commodities, it makes no difference because trend-lines are a usable tool whenever you wish.

In addition to explaining how to use the trend-line indicator, we will provide you with some valid, proven strategic advice from industry experts, therefore by dedicating 5 minutes of your time to reading this strategy, you can achieve excellent results need is a little patience. .

How does the trend-line indicator work?

You will surely already be aware that we don't like to leave anything to chance especially when we explain the operation of a technical indicator. Clarifying is the best way so that once you have finished reading this article, you can go to the financial markets directly to start using the trend-lines and try to make some investments through them. To begin with, therefore, it is really necessary to give a clear and simple definition of the trend-line concept. This indicator has been used since time immemorial in trading and has always offered excellent results to its users.

If you are observing the price trend on a graph and you seem to be able to identify a real trend or a trend within the market, it will be precisely with the trend lines that you will be able to properly highlight the directionality of the market both it is bullish or bearish.

The Italian name of the indicator as we have already mentioned is "trend lines", they are precisely half-lines drawn on a graph when the price moves in a specific direction.

There are, to be precise, 2 distinct types of trend-lines:

Support trend-line: a support trend-line and bullish or bullish trend-line, it is a dynamic support line that joins two or more increasing lows reached by the price.

Resistance trend-line: on the contrary when we talk about a resistance trend-line we refer to a bearish trend line or a bearish trend-line. It is a dynamic resistance line drawn on a graph by joining two or more decreasing maximums reached by the price.

Not all trend-lines should be considered reliable in the same way, a trend line can be considered solid only when it has touched at least two or more points on the price, increasing or decreasing as we have highlighted above.

Opening positions with the trend-line indicator

So let's now find out the most interesting aspect of the use of the trend-lines this means that we are going to offer you some methods of use operating on the trend-line graphs for the opening of purchase or sale positions that are valid for any tool financial you decide to use with the particular expediency to always turn to those lively and highly directional markets, characterized by strong volatility, with particular reference to the Forex market of course and by the main pair of this market the EUR / USD.

The advantage of using this indicator certainly lies in allowing an effective investment both in the long term and in the medium term. Still, ultimately also the operators who prefer investments in intraday trading can benefit enormously from the use of the trend lines that however, they should always be used also with the help of other technical indicators that enrich and optimize the information already obtained through the trend-lines.

Long market entry: you can choose to enter a long market when the breakdown of a resistance trend line occurs, however it will be necessary for the new level of support to be tested by the price without a new breakdown occurring or, an unsuccessful side phase.

Short market entry: on the contrary you can decide to open a bearish position when the breakdown of a support trend-line occurs, in this case the new dominant market forces will be the sellers, but as always wait for the signal to be confirmed by the succession of the highest decreases touched by the price 2-3 times.

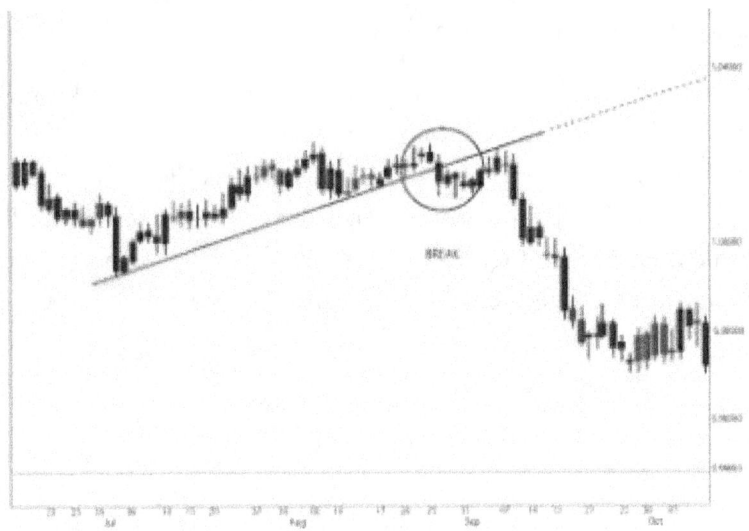

Use the trend-lines to invest and enjoy their ease of use like many other operators before you. Doing technical analysis and earning thanks to your reading skills of the graphs could be much simpler than you thought. By illustrating the functioning of the trendlines we have amply demonstrated it to you now it is up to you to apply these simple principles to get the most out of your performed.

Trading Strategy With The Use Of RSI

Many traders want to scalp but cannot find a valid way that allows them to put the technique into practice to its full potential. It is not easy to find a strategy that can give excellent results in most of the trades that take place. Still, today you have the opportunity to know a scalping strategy that is used a lot and by a large number of investors for the simple fact that everyone understood that it works, but above all nobody has difficulty in putting it into practice.

The RSI oscillator and its operation

In practice this indicator of the relative strength of the price is a useful tool for studying graphs similar to the stochastic. If you want to insert it on your price chart you can see that its standard value is set at 14 periods, but you can change it according to your preferences even if the advice is always to leave it as it is.

If what we have said so far seems complicated to you, just know that the RSI oscillator is nothing more than a line, very similar to a moving average that is lent below your price chart and oscillates between two values: 0 and 100. Between these two values it is possible to indicate two particularly significant areas that you must always keep under close control, the area above the value of 70 and the one below the value of 30.

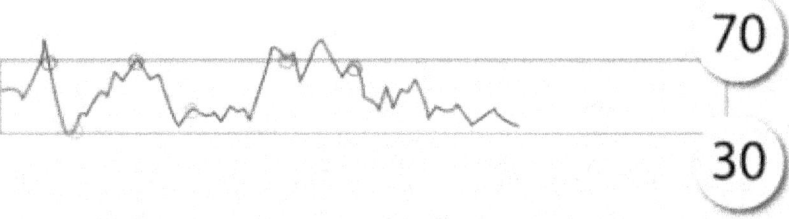

But why are these two areas so important to achieve results using this strategy?

Here we come to the point because it is the key concept of this strategy. In fact, when the RSI is below the value of 30, the security or asset on which you want to trade is in an oversold phase, while when it is above 30 you are in an overbought phase. As you will know in trading, reversals and price corrections are extremely important and very often they represent the only, if not the most important, opportunities to place an investment. This is why it is necessary to pay attention to the overbought and unsold items: when the price is in those areas there may be a reversal of the trend.

A 50 line is also shown in the indicator, which is very useful for identifying the prevailing direction of the market you are analyzing. Especially you have to notice if the line is oscillating from the bottom up or vice versa.

If you want to confirm the real formation of a new trend on the market, you just need to identify a divergence. Divergences are very important in trading because they can offer very reliable signals that lead to successful trading in most cases.

In the graph you can see 2 examples of divergences relating to the RSI oscillator. In the first case we have a rise in the price and a RSI in the descending phase, which indicates that a bearish reversal could occur in the short term, which we actually find in the graph. In the second case, however, we can observe the opposite case: a decrease in the price and a RSI in a bullish phase, here too the same rule applies and therefore the price shortly after begins to rise.

Trading signals with the scalping strategy with RSI

Now that you understand how the RSI indicator works, let us go into more detail to understand how to use the indicator by scalping...

First you need to select a suitable time frame of the chart. Obviously, if you intend to scalp the time frame of the be very narrow and in no case should it exceed 15 minutes.

Remember that with scalping then, and operating at such low time frames, your operation cannot last very long. Some performed remain open even for only a few seconds, up to a maximum of 4-5 minutes, only rarely longer, also because it is very difficult for new trends to last very long on such a short time frame.

Long market entry: a bullish position can be opened when the market is oversold. Therefore below the limit threshold of 30 indicates that the market is not strong enough to continue its bearish direction and a reversal of the trend. Thus, it is imminent and will be bullish.

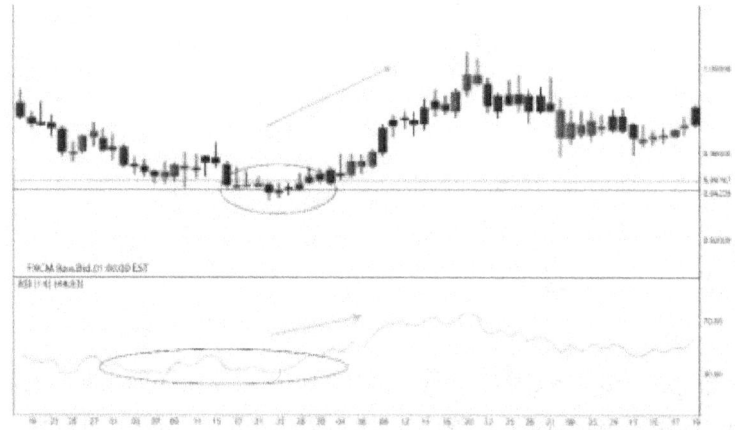

Entry to short market: instead you can earn by opening a short position when the market is in the overbought phase so you will notice that the RSI line moves too high up to exceed the value of 70, so here by force of things the market will change direction because there has been an excess of upward and you can get in and out quickly by taking advantage of the trend correction.

CHAPTER 26:

Currency Futures And Cryptocurrencies

WHAT ARE CURRENCY FUTURES?

Futures markets and easy access to the currency speculation they provide have been around for decades. In this book, I chose to put a little more emphasis on the relatively new and somewhat unknown world of FOREX. However, it is essential that traders fully understand the opportunities available to them in future currency markets. As you will see from this text, I am trying to be a champion of monetary speculation through centralized and regulated futures instead of ready-to-use products (FOREX).

Although the futures market is the most mature, many novice traders are unaware of the possibility of speculating on currencies through futures. Even worse, they are not aware of the benefits of doing so. This is likely because futures markets have been overshadowed by the widespread and aggressive marketing techniques used by foreign exchange dealers to acquire new customers and gain a speculative market share from futures brokers. Nevertheless, currency futures are traded in abundance on the CME Group's Globex Futures trading platform and may offer a more liquid trading environment than most credits.

Like foreign exchange contracts, futures contracts are electronic contracts that create or receive the underlying asset at a particular future date. In other words, the seller of a future contract agrees to deliver the declared goods on a predetermined delivery date; the buyer of a futures contract agrees to receive the goods declared on the stipulated delivery date. The only variable in a futures transaction is the price at which it is made - and buyers and sellers in the market determine it. Traders often underestimate the big difference between traded shares versus leveraged futures trades and FOREX environments. When an equity trader buys part of a particular business, he buys an asset. As the owner of these shares, he is entitled to any future cash flow generated by the share, such as dividends and capital gains (assuming the stock is sold at a profit). Traders and futures do not trade or sell an asset; instead, they negotiate a liability derived from the underlying asset's value; thus, they are known as derivatives.

Unlike foreign exchange contracts, currency futures are delivered only four times a year, according to the quarterly cycle. As you may recall, currency traders technically review deliveries to positions that have been occupied for more than two days but are forced to flip them daily to avoid making or receiving deliveries. Forex traders, on the other hand, only have to worry about rolling positions in March, June, September, and December. Scrolling is simply deleting a contract that expires and entering the next available contract month. For example, a trader bought a futures contract on the yen in December to deliver the underlying asset that was approaching. It would sell a yen in December to exit the position and buy a yen in March to restore a long position. Again, this process is called rollover and must be run manually by the merchant. This is different from FOREX, where the broker automatically launches the customer's positions.

Contract expiration

Now, you know that futures contracts are expiring agreements between buyers and sellers of these contracts to trade the underlying currency. You also know that most speculators have little interest in participating in the delivery process. However, it is a bit more complicated to avoid the delivery obligations inherent in the conclusion of a future contract than to spend the day before your official salary.

The expiry of the contract is the day and time when a given month of maturity of a future foreign exchange contract is no longer negotiated, and the final settlement price is determined. That's when the delivery process begins. Except for a few obscure contracts, CME-listed currency futures are delivered four times a year on the third Wednesday of March, June, September, and December. If there is no holiday or other holidays, the last trading day for the CME coins is the Monday before the expiry date. As a result, traders should be outside their positions well before they expire. Traders who are not interested in creating or receiving the underlying currency should leave their positions on the previous Friday, but preferably before.

The WEC publishes an official renewal date in which traders are advised to move from the due month to the month following the contract. The suggested date for doing this is exactly one week before the last trading day and probably does not prevent hitting the flock. You would not want to hold open positions until the last trading day because the market will likely have declined to this point. This will not only result in wider gaps between supply and demand but may also result in irrational volatility.

As a reminder, foreign exchange renewals occur daily, while renewals of futures contracts occur only four times a year. However, one of the advantages of FX trading is that your broker will automatically roll over your positions without you lifting a finger. A futures broker will not give you the same courtesy. Still, if you negotiate with a legitimate broker, you will do everything possible to inform you of the expiration of the contract and prevent the delivery process from occurring. While this may be among the most common fears among futures traders, accidental possession of positions during delivery is rare. If you make the mistake of triggering delivery, do not panic! It is repairable, but it can cost you a few hundred dollars to give up your obligation. This is something you would like to avoid.

Unlike currency transfers, which involve the inconvenience and potential cost of interest rate differentials, term traders should not be overburdened with credit and interest rates. The commission and the natural spread between the bid and ask minimal prices (usually a tick) are only the cost of a futures contract.

Futures markets have high standards

Without the standardization of contracts, buyers and sellers would be forced to negotiate the details of each transaction. As you can imagine, this would significantly slow down speculation and eliminate liquidity and market efficiency.

Despite significant differences in the size of contracts between futures and foreign exchange contracts, trading in both arenas uses standard contracts that can be easily purchased or sold in any order. In currency futures, there are three standard contract sizes. For example, futures traders have the opportunity to negotiate a full contract that varies in size (except for the yen and the pound sterling) from 100,000 to 125,000 units. A mini-contract is measured at half of the standard, and E-micro futures represent one-tenth of the size of the original futures contract.

How can a futures market guarantee every trade?

Once again, FOREX trades are subject to counterparty risk. If the person or entity that assumes the other part of your foreign exchange transaction cannot fulfill your obligation, you cannot be compensated by specific speculation especially if you trade through a trading desk where your brokerage acts as a market maker. As you can imagine, it is not always able to fulfill its financial obligations. This is especially true if you can accumulate significant profits, resulting in huge losses for the counterparty. Such events are rare in frequency, but I think we can all agree that once, it's too much! It is not because it was not a common problem in the past that this will not happen in the future - and it is difficult to justify taking unnecessary risks in negotiations. It is hard enough to make money in the markets based on controllable factors, not to mention the fate of your trading account for the finances of others. REFCO, the well-known US-based FOREX broker that collapsed in 2005, turns balances into customer accounts in cents after the bankruptcy courts split the remains.

One of the most interesting features of futures is the foreign exchange guarantee. Each transaction canceled by a futures exchange is guaranteed; Unfortunately, such a guarantee does not mean that you will earn money. Instead, it is the guarantee that, if you speculate correctly, you will be compensated for the deserved amount based on the price of entries and exits. Most traders believe that this will always be the case, regardless of the markets they trade and the broker they use, but this is not the case. FOREX traders do not have the same luxury of knowing that market integrity is always protected by applicable rules and regulations.

Although the NFA recently limited the leverage offered by currency brokers, they were free to provide clients with significant leverage. As wonderful as some traders thought it was, that's exactly why currency brokers could never guarantee business; excessive leverage is more risk to the counterparty and the trader. Futures markets stipulate and impose margin requirements for each foreign exchange contract at a rate generally greater than that of similar foreign exchange contracts. This allows them the risk management needed to provide operators with a performance guarantee.

Margin is a necessary nemesis; without ensuring that speculators have sufficient funds in hand to cover potential losses, stock exchanges and futures brokers run the risk that speculators move away from their trading losses to let them hold the purse. Even with the margin required on the deposit, traders can lose more than the funds in their trading account (yes, this is possible with leveraged speculation, and this happens). If this happens, it creates a negative balance on the customer's account, called the balance owing, and gives rise to a chargeable customer of his brokerage firm. As a result, the broker's role has been entrusted to the lender and not to the entity bringing together buyers and sellers. To strengthen the ability of futures markets to secure transactions, it is customary to keep the broker-dealer responsible for covering the client's obligations with the exchange until he can reconstitute the entire account. ... where appropriate.

Term exchanges act as a bank, giving traders access to products of substantial value in exchange for a "payment" or a minimum margin. Fortunately, the rules that are actively enforced concerning the appropriate margin and futures exchanges hold brokerages accountable for their clients' debit balances contribute to market liquidity and stability attempts - a feature that real estate, cannot always portray.

On the contrary, while foreign exchange traders seem less exposed to the risk of counterparty default in the current environment, thanks to NFA's new margin rules which limit leverage to 50 to 1, these gap trading platforms seem to make currency futures much more advantageous. more attractive for FX

Now that we have made it clear that FOREX traders are subject to counterparty risk and that futures traders are not, let's look at the process that allows futures exchanges to guarantee transactions executed with a little more detail. As you know, to establish a position in the US futures market, an operator must have a specific amount of margin on the deposit. If the trader's positions change unfavorably to trigger a margin call, an adjustment, settlement, or deposit of funds is required to continue the speculative game.

CHAPTER 27:

Easy Ways to Reduce Your Risks

Trading in the Forex market can be risky. There are a lot of different options to choose from since the market is open 24-hours a day, and you have to worry not only about the two currencies that you want to trade in but also about other countries that interact with your chosen countries. All of this can mean a lot of risk on your part. The good news is that there are some easy things that you can do to ensure that you reduce your risks and see great results in the end.

Research the Economies You Want to Invest In

Research is so important when it comes to picking out the right currency pairs. Not only do you need to worry about the two currencies that you want to work with, but you also have to worry about any countries that trade with those countries, and how changes in that country will affect your trade.

You should never just jump into a trade when you join the Forex market. Steady research, including before, during, and after the trade, can make a big difference in the results that you see. Pick out the newspapers, magazines, and other resources that you want to use and then read through them on a regular basis.

And always make sure that at least one of your sources gives you daily news so you can keep up with what is happening around you and if any big events will change the value of your currency pair.

Keep the Emotions at Home

Emotions are going to be a deal breaker with any investment. As soon as you allow the emotions to come into the game, things are going to head downhill for you. These emotions can get in the way of clear thinking and often cause you to lose a lot of extra money in the Forex market. Learning how to keep the emotions out of your trades is critical if you would like to make a profit in the process.

This is why it's so important to have a solid trading plan from the beginning. That way, when you enter the market, you know exactly what you will invest in, how long you plan to invest, what needs to happen for you to leave the market, and more. And as long as you stick with that plan, you should be able to limit any potential losses and even help yourself make more money in the Forex market overall.

If you are someone who often falls prey to their emotions, then it may be best to consider a different form of trading. Emotions will force you into revenge trading, staying in the market for too long, speculation, and other behaviors that are risky and can make you lose a lot of money. Sticking with a good trading plan and trading strategy can make the difference in how successful you are with this market though.

Work with a Broker

As a beginner, it is a good idea to work with a broker. The Forex market can be confusing sometimes and having a professional by your side, someone who can answer any of your questions and who will walk you through some of the steps can be a game saver. Add in that brokers often have the platforms that you need, at least the good and secure ones, and it makes sense that you would want to work with a good broker.

Before you pick a broker though, make sure to discuss their fees and any other information with them. Some brokers charge based on how much you trade in the market, and some will charge a flat fee. You will also be charged more or less depending on how much help you need from the broker in the process. Have a listing of all the fees ahead of time so you know how much of your profits will go to someone else.

Put Your Stop Losses in Place

Always make sure that you have your stop losses in place when you begin to trade. These will ensure that you keep your losses to a minimum and help you to keep any of your profits as well. These stop points tell the market when you want to exit, even if you are asleep and can't watch your computer all the time. The stop losses can do a great job of keeping you in the game, limiting your losses, and preventing more risk than is necessary.

First, you must step a stop loss for losing money. This needs to be placed at the point where you are comfortable losing that much money. When the market goes down and reaches that point, your trade will be closed, and you will just have to settle that loss. Even if the market continues to go down, your stop loss took you out and ensured you didn't lose more money.

If you had gotten into the market without the stop loss, you might have wanted to stay in the market and hoped that things got better. Or the downturn may have happened while you were asleep, and you wouldn't be able to fix the issue. Either way, this stop loss can help save you a bunch of money.

You should also put in a stop loss for your profits as well. This will be at the place where you are most comfortable with the profits that you make. Doing this ensures that if the stock reaches that certain point, you will be able to walk away with a profit. This way, if you are away from the computer for some reason, and the currency hits your profit point, but then takes a sharp turn down, you get to take the profit because the system took you out before the downturn occurred. This helps you to maintain your profits and can-do wonders for keeping your emotions out of the game.

Never Revenge Trade

Revenge trading can take all of your hard work and throws it down the drain. With revenge trading, the investor often loses money in a trade, and it is usually a significant amount. After losing that money, they panic and decide to try to earn it all back as quickly as possible. They make a succession of bad trading decisions, don't stick with their trading plan, and run into a lot more trouble. Since the investor is not really taking care of their money or the way that they spend it, they end up losing more money in the long run.

Never fall prey to revenge trading. Even after losing money, which is something that everyone runs into at some point or another, just restart and do your trading just like normal. If you find this too hard to accomplish because you got emotionally tied into a trade, this is fine. Just make sure you stop trading for at least a few days and take a break. Once you have regrouped and feel a bit better, and know that you can make good decisions, you can come back and trade the market again.

Find a Mentor to Work With

This can be your broker or someone else you trust and who has spent some time investing in the past. You may find that working with someone who has direct experience in the Forex market is the best but working with someone who has invested at all can make a big difference. This person is perfect to ask questions of, to test out strategies with, and to get some help when things seem tough with your trades.

Most people will be happy to help you with your trades. Just remember to be respectful of the time they are giving you. You may want to bring along some questions and concerns to the meeting and use those to keep the flow of the conversation going. This ensures that you get all of your questions done, without taking up too much time from the individual who agreed to be your mentor.

Of course, you are the trader in this market, and it is your money that is on the line. While your mentor is going to give you some good advice (if you pick the right mentor), you also have to think through the process ahead of time and make sure that any advice makes sense for what you want to do. If you feel that another trade would work better, or you are not comfortable taking that much risk, even if it is recommended by a good mentor, then you don't have to do it.

A good trader can think critically for themselves, and while they appreciate the advice and help, they get from others, it is still important to think through things on your own and consider whether they make sense for your investment or not.

Take a Break When Needed

It can be hard sometimes, but you need to know when it's time to take a break from trading. If you are making a series of bad trades in the market, if you happen to lose a lot of money on one trade, or you just can't seem to get really good results at all, then it may be time to take a break and try again after a few weeks or so have passed.

The problem with staying in the market during these situations is that your thinking is going to become clouded in many cases. The more that you lose, the more that you struggle, the harder it will be to make the decisions that are needed for trading. Taking a few weeks off to clear the head and then coming back fresh can be one of the best decisions that you can make.

Do Not Invest with More Than You Can Afford to Lose

Many traders fall into the trap of investing more than they can really afford to lose. This can be really tempting for those who want to use leverage to make their positions a bit stronger. Unless you have been in the market for some time, it is not a good idea to trade on leverage. This is just asking for the market to go the opposite way of your prediction and can make you lose out on a lot of money in the process.

It is always risky to invest more money than you can afford to lose. Often, the investor will make rash decisions or will decide not to do the right research, and this can result in a disaster. It is much better to figure out how much you can comfortably lose, in case the position is wrong, and then only invest that much. It may limit the amount of profit that you can earn, but it ensures that you aren't left without options and scrounging for the money at the end.

While there is always going to be a little bit of risk when it comes to trading on the Forex market, there are some ways that you can help to reduce the risk and ensure that you see some great results.

Conclusion

Thank you for making it to the end. If your forex targets are ambitious (such that it will come to represent an essential component of your income or even the lion's share), then you should treat forex as though it were a company. You'll need to adopt an organized approach, in other words. Forex shouldn't be something you seek to get in whenever you feel like it; instead, you should strive to set aside a specific amount of time and incorporate forex into your daily routine. It would help if you devoted your time solely to education and research, unlike when you trade and track your account. Ideally, you might want to leave this kind of homework for the weekends if you are not distracted by live markets and the possibility of doing business.

Always remember that multiple factors affect the forex market. That is the reason why forex traders usually rely on technical analysis. With so many factors that influence the prices of different currencies, it becomes almost impossible to predict the price movement of money. Of course, you can always apply an effective strategy, but it does not change the fact that the forex market is challenging, if not impossible, to predict.

A business also needs its own space. You might also consider getting a separate computer devoted exclusively to forex-related operations, depending on your forex regime's rigor. Forex isn't like your 9-to-5 job, which is probably interrupted by checking your Facebook account and espn.com frequently. It's Forex time when your laptop computer is powered on.

Ultimately, you'll have to control your forex company finances. All expenses should be reported with due care, and you should try to measure the return on investment for all costs, including this book!

You will conduct an analysis of your account at monthly, quarterly, and yearly intervals. You will display the productivity and efficiency metrics in real-time if you maintain a trading log. Did the result fulfill your expectations? If so, consider withdrawing from your account a fraction of your profits so that your earnings become real, not just digital. If your performance has been unsatisfactory, what can you do to make it better?

Remember, it will take time for your forex business to develop, as is the case with any new business. Give yourself a reasonable time in which you hope to succeed. Profits won't come immediately, but your forex company will one day be able to stand on its own two feet with hard work!

Success in Forex trading needs not only research but also understanding, not only preparation but also execution, not only achieving profits but also minimizing losses. Luckily, now you're well on your way to being an expert or becoming a good currency trader.

Our main adjective in writing this book was to provide you with a robust framework and base of knowledge to interact with the forex trading. Then it is up to you to apply for your experience. Good luck and take things slowly. I hope you have learned something!

Bonus Chapter

Forex Robots

One of the best ways to make a passive income from the forex market is using a tool known as a forex robot, which performs automated trades on a trader's behalf. Once traders set up these forex robots, they do not have to do much else; however, they should keep an eye on the trades the forex robots are making for them. To get started, traders need to perform adequate research into the software available for forex robots. They need to choose software that will meet their needs, in addition to being reliable when it comes to executing the right forex trades. After setting up this software, it will make forex trades based on preset signals. In addition, it will use its acquired knowledge to purchase or sell at specific times, earning users a passive income in the process. However, it is important to understand that not all forex robots make passive income for investors as claimed. In the same way that a human can make a losing trade, a forex robot can also make the same mistake. It is also important to understand that many so-called forex robots are frauds, which is why respected news platforms such as the Wall Street Journal and Forbes refuse to promote or advertise them. Unfortunately, this is particularly true when it comes to free forex robots. Therefore, new forex traders should analyze testimonials and reviews carefully before entrusting their investment to a forex robot.

Fortunately, several leading sites focus on reviewing different trading platforms. These sites try to give an honest opinion of different investment platforms and outline all the benefits and limitations of each platform. They also offer a detailed analysis of how these platforms work and how traders can get started on them, which is especially helpful to new traders.

How To Program The Metatrader 4 To Automate The Management Of Operations With A Custom Trading Console

There are many benefits in an automated trading system and most of them are centered around saving time, reducing stress and so on. For example, when a trader knows that the system will be sending him/her an alert when a new trade signal is generated, he/she can go about doing something else such as spending time with the family or preparing for the next day's work. Other benefits include easy maintenance of your program or code, reduced space for errors and so on.

The Meta Trader 4 programming language has been around for a while and many expert programmers have come up with huge number of programs to suit various trading styles. However with time as we get more familiar with MQL4 , it becomes easier to write our own programs. One fantastic thing about MQL4 is that anything you type can be auto compiled into binary code and executed just like any other program even without compilation which we will see towards the end of this article. So if you are going to learn programming in Metatrader 4, then let us start by learning how to program GUI based indicators and then we can move on to advanced topics like algo trading.

MT4 GUI based indicators are a great way to start learning programming in MQL4. Most professionals will choose to start with a simple indicator such as the MACD. It is not necessary that you have to use the MACD as a jumping off point; you can create any sort of indicator using the GUI. Once you are comfortable with that, then it's time to move on and create our own indicators which will help us make money out of the market. These types of indicators (GUI based) have inbuilt alerts which send updates in real time and this gives us a great advantage over other traders who don't know how to program their own automation system at all.

If you are new to Metatrader 4 programming, then gaining proficiency in creating these types of indicators should be your first priority because they have a lot more features than those based on price bar charts.

MT4 can be made automated by writing in-built functions called MQL4 prog. So instead of using the GUI to build your indicators, you can use that available programming language using which you will write every piece of code for the indicator i.e. graphical representation, alerts and so on. To write a function using MT4 prog, all we have to do is create a file with extension "prog" and then name it accordingly (ex: "ADX" would be an example). Once we create the file, we have to right click on it from the Meta Trader's main menu bar and select "Properties". From here, select all tabs except 'Security' tab which needs confirmation before being changed as shown below: There are two types of programming languages in Meta Trader 4 graphical user interface (GUI) e-charting section: One is simple scripting language and other is advanced scripting language which also compiles into binary code making it operational. The simple scripting language allows programmers to code any parameter they wish but if you want to program advanced features like algo trading or exporting data into other platforms such as Excel or TradingStation etc.

some practical example include :

Simple scripting language:

Programmer can code any parameter they wish. Theoretically it can be used to program any indicator or strategy.

simple example: "if(state==1,price<1,0,"+")"

Advanced scripting language: this programming language also compiles into binary code which is operational and can be used directly in a trading account with no need for compilation.

some practical examples:

Note that the above two programming languages are the same as simple scripting language but are more advanced and compiled into binary code.

Actually all of MQL4 programming languages are the same type of programming language (simple scripting) except one which is compiled into binary code and is operational.

In simple scripting language, we use a combination of mainly two characters to create a program: "If" and "EndIf". For example: if price > range then put order in trade box else put order in profit box. These programmed scripts can be saved with different names like "MySignals1", "MySignals2", etc. A sample of the script would look like this :

if(state == 1,price < 1, 0,"+")

This will work as long as no other variables were added to this script after creating it or if another script was added with different names. This program is limited to what you can code it for and they can not be used for complicated algorithms or any advanced strategy trading because these require compilation into binary code which we will see later on how to do it using Metatrader4 prog. An example of un-compiled script for simple alert box is shown below:

if(state == 1,price > 1,0,"+")

In this case output will be "+" because price is greater than 1.

Advanced scripting language is more advanced and can be used to write any kind of indicator or strategy. It uses the same "If" and "EndIf", but the difference between simple programming language and advanced programming languages is that in advance languages are compiled into binary code to make it operational without any need for compilation.

A simple example of an advanced script with an ADX indicator can be seen below:

static void MA_ADX(int period1, double price1, int period2, double price2, string name) { double   Adx1   =   iMA(NULL   ,   0 ,period1,price1);   double   Adx2   =   iMA(NULL   ,   0 ,period2,price2); return Adx1 - Adx2; }

Compiling MQL4 prog files : All .

Machine Learning For Algorithmic Trading

Trading now contributes significantly to the wealth of individuals and companies globally. It is not surprising that many people want to cash in on this opportunity for increased wealth. At the same time, algorithmic trading and machine learning has become a hot area in finance. The availability of open source machine learning libraries and access to cheap computational power has made it easier for an individual or a company to apply machine learning techniques to trading problems.

However, while applying machine learning methods to trading problems is becoming increasingly popular, there are many issues that need to be addressed, not least the fact that researchers and practitioners have yet to agree on what constitutes best practice in this area.

Machine learning is typically concerned with creating models that are based on historical data and that can be used to predict future outcomes. The accuracy of any model is dependent on the quality of the historical data set. When dealing with financial instruments, there are two main issues:

This poses a particular problem when dealing with longer time series of data, as problems such as these can be difficult to avoid.

This issue has recently been highlighted by research from TABB Group (Tabb Group 2015). They have noted that out-of-sample testing shows a risk to the performance of long-short stock trading strategies since February 2000, and that for the top ten firms in this study, out-of-sample forecasting increases from roughly 80% in 2012 to about 90% in 2014 (TABB Group 2015). While it is interesting that their results show what they claim are "decreasing returns" over time for these strategies (Zeiler 2013), it should not be assumed that this is necessarily due to a failure of machine learning methods; rather this is more likely an indication of significant changes in financial markets over the past few years.

The fact remains that, for most financial data sets, there are significant issues with the in-sample and out-of-sample data sets. Machine learning, however, is not limited to dealing with the historical aspect of financial data; it also has something to offer when it comes to capturing the complexity of financial time series.

While an important research area in its own right (Geman et al 2015, Dacorogna et al 2002), machine learning can be applied not only to predicting future values of securities but also to the identification of structural changes in these values – such as market crashes (Wüthrich 2004). For example, LeBaron et al (LeBaron et al 2008) applied machine learning methods to the identification of market crashes in several of the global stock markets. They found that by using machine learning approaches they could successfully detect market changes with a significant impact on specific stocks.

In addition, there is increasing interest in developing strategies that can automatically rebalance portfolios based on expected returns and risks (Reeve 2014). To do this, one needs to develop strategies that are able to make decisions based on both historical and real-time data. Since many stock exchanges do not have complete historical data sets, it is difficult to use purely historical data for making trading decisions. Therefore, it becomes useful to develop systems capable of making decisions based on both historical and real-time data – such as when dealing with tick data (i.e., high frequency financial time series).

Automatic trading systems can be developed using machine learning through the use of components such as artificial neural networks (ANNs), support vector machines (SVMs), random forests, or k-nearest neighbours.

DAY Trading diary

Day trading is a form of active trading of stocks, futures, options and other securities. It is the use of short-term price movements for profit where the goal is not long-term growth.

Trading can rarely be called "day" because "day traders" are typically in and out of positions within a few hours (when working from home or off-hours). Though most trades are completed in less than a day, it may take days or weeks for the resulting position to be realized by closing out the trade.

Light trading volume is considered to be less than 50% of a stock's average daily volume. A high trading volume suggests a strong interest in the stock and usually, therefore, a high price volatility. High trading volumes also suggest a greater liquidity of stocks.

The risk associated with day trading is substantial, like gambling, and day traders can and do lose all their capital in short periods of time or suffer large losses from price volatility.

Day traders may employ chart analysis or use computer programs that can assist in making buy/sell decisions. Many day traders also trade using technical analysis by downloading price quotes from a financial data service provider or an exchange, and use programs that display the resulting data in charts. The technical analysis can help the trader figure out optimal times for entering into positions as well as getting an idea about the overall trend of prices. Day traders will often have several positions open at once (commonly called "leverage" — on margin) which allows them to have greater exposure to the market while not having to put up as much capital as they otherwise would need to maintain their positions if they were not using leverage or maintaining such open positions for longer periods of time.

Stock exchanges and most futures exchanges operate on a principle of "last price/time traded" for reporting prices. Such price quotes will show up on the ticker tape or on data sites as bid and offer prices, which are the last price at which a trading bid was made or an offer made to buy, and the last price at which a bid was made at ask or an offer to sell. These prices are known as "inside market" or "spot" prices. The inside market is essentially determined by only one bid and ask: the highest bid and lowest ask. For active day traders this is critical information in determining price direction because it reflects the true supply and demand of securities at any given moment in time, and reveals how close buyers or sellers may be to the supply/demand level (also known as support and resistance levels).

In order to maintain a position over time, day traders are constantly monitoring current market activity by looking for changes in current opinion about value which would indicate new momentum in either direction based upon a continuing increase in buyer interest (demand) or continuing decrease in buyer interest (supply), respectively.